EXECUTOR HELP

How to Settle an Estate

Pick an Executor and Avoid Family Fights

DAVID E. EDEY

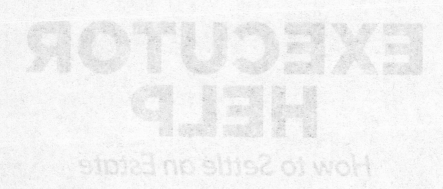

FriesenPress

Suite 300 - 990 Fort St
Victoria, BC, V8V 3K2
Canada

www.friesenpress.com

ISBN
978-1-03-910727-4 (Hardcover)
978-1-03-910726-7 (Paperback)
978-1-03-910728-1 (eBook)

1. REFERENCE, HANDBOOKS & MANUALS

Distributed to the trade by The Ingram Book Company

Contents

Contents

Dedication

To my mom and dad — I miss your voices every day.

To my sister Velma — I'm sharing our story. As painful, frustrating and as costly it was, we got through it.

We did our best to look after Mom and Dad when they needed us the most, despite the interference from family members who did nothing to help.

We know who our true family is.

I love you.

Hopefully, others will learn from us and be able keep their family together.

To my only family – Terry, Dawn, Myles, and the next generation, Jasmyn and Isiah, I love you and appreciate you all.

To my son Spencer – I know you are going to do great things. The world is waiting for you.

And to my partner in crime and life, Susan – You will never know how far my love will go. I appreciate all the sacrifices you made to change my life. You mean so much to me. I wish the world could see all the joy you bring to my life. I would do anything for you.

Introduction

My nightmare began when my mom died in 2011 and less than a year later, my dad was gone too.

There is not a day that goes by that I do not miss hearing their voices.

Little did I know it would take seven years, ten court appearances, mediation, $50,000 in lawyer fees, and double bypass heart surgery for my nightmare to end.

And my parents had a will.

Anytime I would talk about my grief, disappointment, and anger with friends or clients, I would learn about one more estate that had gone wrong or the frustrations they had gone through being an executor.

The more I heard these kinds of stories, the more I wanted to help others. I did not want others to go through what my sister and I did. So, I decided to write this book

A study done by the Canadian Imperial Bank of Commerce found 84 per cent of respondents have named a friend or family member as executor.

However, about 80 per cent of respondents who were named as executor had no prior experience in administering a will.

The survey also found that two-thirds of Canadians thought an estate could be wrapped up in a year or less, while 38 per cent thought that it would take less than six months.

In reality, if all goes smoothly, you'll be spending more than 100 hours of your time and from twelve to eighteen months to wrap up an estate. And complications such as tax errors can delay the process by months or even years.

The goal of *Executor Help* is threefold.

1. Point out the often-unforeseen biggest challenges and concerns in becoming an executor.

2. Give you a step-by-step explanation, along with tips, strategies, and actual client stories, including some celebrity ones, for you to understand what the job involves.

3. And, finally, keep you from spending $50,000 or having to take time out for heart surgery in between court appearances.

You don't need to read the book chapter by chapter. You can go directly to the sections you need help and understanding with.

This book is not a substitute for professional accounting, legal, and financial advice. You are going to need a team.

But you'll be prepared and organized to help them do their jobs, which will save you time and money.

This is about finding the best way to get an estate settled in the shortest period of time with the least amount of headache and stress.

Having gone through the process myself, I know that settling an estate can change family dynamics forever. Mine did

I am going to be honest with you—this is not an easy job.

After reading this book, you will know how to plan your estate and pick an executor because you will now understand what the job is all about and be able to prepare them.

Chapter 1
How to handle your grief

Nicole, Cameron, and Julia need clarity and help. They have just lost their mother after a battle with cancer.

The grief is heavy for them. Fortunately, they were able to be with her at the end.

Now they must plan a funeral, deal with friends and relatives from all over the country, and have their final goodbye.

How do they cope with their grief and sense of loss?

What can they do to help them get some peace and prepare to do all the tasks required to settle the estate?

How do they get through the visit to the house and go through their mother's things?

In my case, it is still all a painful blur to remember the events on that morning of March 29, 2011. I received a phone call at home to head down to the hospital right away. My mom was gone.

I feel so fortunate I got to say my goodbye to her the day before, but little did I know then that it would be the last time I would talk to her. Her children, family members, and close friends—hadn't left her bedside for eight straight days, and that night had been the first time I had slept in my bed in days.

Even though she knew she was leaving us, her sense of humor during those final days was still there. She was always trying to make us feel better.

Until she could no longer talk to us.

That was the kind of woman she was—kind and funny. And she loved her family fiercely.

Then, almost a year later, my dad was gone too. Cancer once again.

So, in less than a year, my two siblings and I became orphans.

Since my parents' death, the assets they earned are no longer owned by the three of us, and we have not celebrated a holiday together as a complete family.

My parents left us behind, unprepared to live life without them.

Then, again, is a child ever prepared never to see their parents again?

My siblings struggled with their own issues, and one of them was never willing to do the right thing.

I foolishly believed that since we were all being treated equally under the terms of our parents' will, there would be no reason for an estate fight. What could be fairer than being treated equally?

You always have to remember that there's the business side to being an executor, and then there's the emotional side of it.

And the two will overlap, especially when talking about your parents and the estate to strangers.

Going to court is never the answer, even if it may seem like a good idea at the time.

But when you are dealing with an unreasonable party, you end up being pushed to do things that would horrify your parents.

How can you prepare to complete the job?

What can you do to not end up fighting with each other and prevent yourselves from damaging relationships forever?

How do you do all this and cope with the sense of loss?

Psychologist Marianne Van Oyen says Nicole, Cameron, and Julia thankfully had the courage and generosity to be with their mother until her last breath.

No one should be forced to do so; however, it will aid in the healing process.

Hopefully, they knew what their mother's final wishes were. That would help alleviate the burden of having to decode them, especially when others might want to chip in their two cents' worth of unsolicited advice. (My siblings and I got plenty of that.)

Van Oyen also says those grieving need to understand that the shock of their loss will help them get things done, and they should capitalize on this energy, even though they will be feeling that everything is surreal.

They should delegate some tasks to other family members to lighten their load, if they can.

Anything will help. They should be clear with the funeral home etc., and family and friends the family/ friends concerning the plans and arrangements.

They should try to have friends and family around for the first few days or even a week following the death, for extra love and support.

Those grieving should try recording their thoughts, memories, and feelings in a journal.

Active grieving is a productive way to grieve, but they should not spend more than an hour in each grieving session, and they should make sure to do something positive or constructive after the session so as not to fall apart and slump into a depression.

Van Oyen advises them to make or get a checklist of what needs to be done. Then divide up the tasks and speak together once or twice a week to keep each other in the loop.

They should:

- Take breaks from visits and friends.
- Rest.
- Sleep.
- Eat nutritious food.
- Go for walks to clear their heads.
- Be in nature and plan a getaway, if possible, for when every-thing is settled.
- Go through items carefully and don't get rid of things hastily. But also, don't take too long and get stuck and burdened by the process.
- Arrange with goodwill organizations to pick up items.
- Promise the other siblings to work together as a family and remember that their mother would want them to get along.

- Make a date for six to twelve months in the future to sit together and distribute heirlooms, jewelry, art work, etc., and take turns choosing items to make it fair.
- Seek help from a therapist if they cannot cope individually or as a group, and even consider animal therapy.

According to intuitive animal healer Lesley Nase, animals are also a great help for people who are so overwhelmed by hurt and feelings of loss.

Animals—especially horses, cats, and dogs—have a great way of healing people. The purr of a cat is a vibration that goes straight to your heart and helps it heal.

A dog will sit near or on you when it knows you're feeling sad, and its face, as science has demonstrated, will show real empathy. It will reach out and touch you with its paw.

Nase adds that if you have an animal in your life when you're grieving, you are forced to get up every day to feed it and take care of it. You have to clean its litter, walk it, and pay attention to it. If it is a dog or a horse, it forces you out in nature.

And just being connected with nature is very soothing to the soul. Having a pet in your life alleviates loneliness and gives you somebody to talk to.

That's why, during COVID-19, so many people adopted animals. It made them feel less alone.

Once you are feeling better, it is time to focus on getting the estate settled.

The Executor Help Solution

The biggest dangers and problems that cause stress:

- Not taking the time to grieve.
- Not resting.
- Not eating right

What you need to do:

- Get a journal to start recording your thoughts, memories, and feelings.
- Make a checklist of what needs to be done.
- Seek help from a therapist if you cannot cope individually or as a group.
- Consider getting a pet.

How this helps:

- Your family needs to see itself as a single unit. Working together will strengthen your relationships now and in the future.

For more information on how to handle grief, go to the resources page at www.davidedey.com/resources

5 things you can learn about estate planning in a pandemic

1. Although it's never too early for estate planning, it can be too late.
2. The pandemic has shown us how we react when there is a crisis
3. You're never too old or too young for estate planning.
4. You don't need to have a lot of money to have an estate plan.
5. Expect the unexpected.

Chapter 2
The three goals of being an executor

Amy was named executor of her mother's estate. She had no idea what she had to do.

There were two other siblings, a brother and a sister. Both resented the fact their mother made only the older sister executor.

The estate was to be divided into three equal parts.

There was a family home, pension accounts, and investments to be liquidated, and tax returns to be filed.

An estate can take a few months to a few years to be settled.

This did not sit well with the beneficiaries, and they were constantly requesting their share of the estate and threatening Amy with legal action.

To avoid the kinds of problems Amy had:

1. File the right kind of tax return
2. Pay the taxes on time
3. In Canada: get the clearance certificate
In the United States: to officially close an estate, you'll need to work with a probate court to finalize the process

These are basically the three goals that you have to always keep in mind if you want to settle the estate with the least amount of stress and financial penalties, and without getting sued.

1. File the right kind of tax return.

When someone dies, two taxpayers are created.

First, the income they earned from January 1 of the year of death to the date of death is reported on what is known as the terminal return.

Second, the date after death is the first date for the new taxpayer, which is the estate.

As an executor in Canada, you are responsible for filing T1 personal tax returns on behalf of the deceased, including the terminal tax return.

If the deceased had not filed their tax return for the prior year before their death, you may also have to file a T1 return.

If the tax returns are filed incorrectly, costly government fines could be assessed, money wasted, and family discord fueled.

It's important to remember that taxes might need to be filed for two years, not one.

So, for example: say that Amy's mother died on March 21, 2020, and she did not file her 2019 tax return before she died.

Normally, her 2019 tax return would be due on April 30, 2020.

However, because of her death, Amy doesn't have to file her mother's 2019 tax return until September 21, 2020.

Terminal or Final T1 Return

The tax return for the deceased in the year of their death is called the terminal or final T1 return.

If the testator dies between January 1st and October 31st, the executor must file the deceased's terminal return by April 30th of the following year.

For deaths occurring in November or December, the executor must file the terminal tax return within six months of the testator's death.

Amy's mother died on March 21, 2020, so Amy had to file her terminal T1 return by April 30, 2021. Had she died, for example, on December 22, 2020, Amy would have had to file the terminal T1 return by June 22, 2021.

Christopher was not asked to be one of the executors of his godmother's estate in advance. He only found out that he was by text from the other co-executor on the morning of her death.

His grandmother had lived in a home for many years and had suffered from Alzheimer's. He was told, "If you don't want to be an executor, you can decline," but Christopher accepted because he knew she didn't have any children. He knew he was not going to inherit anything.

There were some other nieces, but none of them were close to her. He didn't know what he was getting involved with.

As executor, you may have to rely on up to seventeen professionals to get the job done.

One of your best decisions at the beginning is to hire a lawyer to handle legal documents and head off any potential conflict with impatient beneficiaries.

It does not take much before a beneficiary wants to go court. This can be due to:

A disagreement over funeral arrangements

- Belief the executor is working too slowly
- Questions about how fit you are to be the executor
- Belief that the executor is undervaluing assets
- Belief that the executor is hiding something and not keeping records

You will also need a chartered accountant, to handle tax issues and keep the estate handling transparent, and a financial adviser to provide wealth preservation advice.

One of the most common reasons accusations arise is the belief that there has been mismanagement on the part of the executor.

If you don't disclose what you are doing, everyone suspects you of wrongdoing.

Secrecy is usually the biggest cause for family feuds, so be up front and transparent with everything you do.

Bringing an accountant into the mix when working as an executor will simplify your job. The accountant makes sure the estate monies are properly handled and tax returns are properly prepared. Most importantly, they minimize your liability.

Be sure to establish the hourly rate, but also what they will do prior to having a good tax professional prepare any work for you.

It would be terrible, both for you and your accountant, to have an initially positive relationship sour upon receipt of that first bill, purely on the basis of a misunderstanding.

How can an accountant help you?

An accountant with estate settling experience can manage the deceased's accounts while the estate is being closed, pay bills, oversee the selling of any goods, and deposit any refunds or over payments, etc.

Having a professional in this role can help prevent any concerns among the beneficiaries that you might be spending money improperly or not managing checking and savings accounts in the right way.

Don't have an accountant?

Ask friends for a referral or do some research online.

Get a feeling if this a person you believe you can work with to get the estate handled professionally and as quickly as possible.

Don't be afraid to shop around, but don't spend a lot of time.

The longer you take, the more it opens you up to criticism from family members and beneficiaries. And it might be seen as you delaying the process.

Make sure the accountant is

1. Open to answering questions in a way that is clear and understandable, so that it is easy for you to pass on the information to the other beneficiaries, should they have questions.

2. Since you could be acting as a middle man between accountant and family, you will want to make sure the accountant can explain things to you in an easy-to-understand way.
3. Be open to talking to the beneficiaries directly, if needed.

2. Distribute to the beneficiaries

As a general rule of thumb, you as the executor should work toward wrapping up the estate within one year of the testator's death.

You could be penalized, personally, if you take too long to get everything completed.

As executor, you assume a certain degree of personal liability when taking on the role. This has to be understood by the beneficiaries. This is where open communication is very important.

Be up front with what is happening with the estate and how it is progressing.

Leaving them out of the process can lead to needless tension, conflict, and sometimes legal action.

3. Close the Estate

Before distributing all of the estate, as executor you should obtain a clearance certificate from the Canada Revenue Agency (CRA). Getting a clearance certificate provides protection for the executor—it does not prevent the CRA from going back to the beneficiaries to get any additional tax that may be owed. However, if you are the executor and the beneficiary, getting a clearance certificate may not be required. But when there is more than one executor and beneficiary, a clearance certificate should be obtained.

The final responsibility of the executor is the same in the United States—to officially close the estate.

This can only be done once all of the beneficiaries have received their legal property, and once taxes and other debts have been paid.

In order to officially close an estate in the United States, you'll need to work with a probate court to finalize the process.

If you distribute all of the estate before receiving government clearance, you can be held personally liable for any additional taxes assessed against the estate.

Christopher's godmother had multiple rental properties and, due to her illness, they were in need of serious repair. She was also behind in paying her taxes.

There was another co-executor, Andre, who was one of the beneficiaries and Raven, who was the other beneficiary. But it was Christopher who did most of the legwork to get the paperwork in order.

Plus, he was taking care of all the properties, collecting rents, tenant requests, etc. He looked after the property, even though he was not going to inherit.

It needed a roof. It needed foundation work. It needed fixing right away.

He was able to do all that using some of the money from the estate that was left in the bank accounts. He was paying the bills for the work to be done.

The biggest issue there was that it was taking a long time.

Raven could not wait and decided to take Christopher and Andre to court.

It was her belief the executors were taking too long to settle the estate and were hiding things.

The court case took a long time, and Christopher and Andre had to attend all the hearings.

Christopher and Andre had to counter-sue because they asked Raven to help out with some money for the property she was about to inherit, as it was falling apart.

She refused, so the judgment was that the house had to be sold.

That, too, took a while. When the property sold, Christopher would get back his money that he had spent.

Raven ended up with less money, nowhere near what she would have received if she had waited.

It was always her belief she was not getting the property she had inherited fast enough.

Christopher said he and Andre tried to explain the situation, but she did not want to listen. Her solution was to go to court.

They couldn't just release the property due to the unpaid taxes, which needed to be settled first.

The Executor Help Solution

The biggest dangers and problems that cause stress:

- Do the job right the first time.
- File the estate's tax return(s) and pay the right amount of taxes.
- Obtain a clearance certificate from Canada Revenue Agency or a judgment from the probate court in the U.S.
- Stay in communication with the beneficiaries on a regular basis so they know that once the tax issues are complete and you have the certificate, they can expect to receive their inheritance.

What you need to do:

- Create your initial team of professionals, which includes a lawyer.
- Find an accountant you feel comfortable working with and who is willing to talk with beneficiaries, if necessary.
- Gather up all the financial information the accountant will need to complete the tax returns professionally.
- Find a financial adviser to help you manage the assets until they are distributed.

How this helps you:

- You have a reliable professional who can not only do the tax returns and speak with beneficiaries, but also act as your voice when speaking with the government on all tax matters related to the estate.

Chapter 3
The truth about being chosen as an executor

Before their family was torn apart, Greg, Robert, and Sandra grew up in a middle-class home.

Their hardworking parents did their best and their children never lacked for anything.

Plus, there was always love and laughter. Fred, the father, was a truck driver, and his wife, Lenora, worked in a factory not far from the family home.

All three children made their own way in the world, with varying degrees of success.

One of the sons, Robert, became concerned as he saw his parents getting older, nearing retirement and not having their affairs in order.

He wanted to talk to them about estate planning.

These conversations are never easy because no one wants to talk about death, especially with their children, and no child wants to discuss their parents' death with them.

In the book *When Roles Reverse: A Guide to Parenting Your Parents*, author Jim Comer writes how the tightrope adult children have to walk can be scary.

> To parent our parents successfully, we must first
> realize that they need our help.
> While denial is natural, there are times we need
> to take the initiative and risk causing raised voices

and tears. It's better to cause a scene than to ignore the truth.

Never minimize the effects of aging and loss.

After my dad had moved out of the house for safety reasons, I remember driving my mom to the supermarket one day and casually bringing up the idea that she live with my sister, who was excited to have Mom go live with her.

I will never forget the amount of tears my mother shed. It broke my heart.

I never brought up the subject again. In the end, it leaves you in a quandary.

Should you do the right thing, step in, and take over, or do nothing so there are no hurt feelings?

There is going to be more on how to talk to your loved ones in an upcoming chapter.

Even though Robert was uncomfortable, I gave him some points to cover. I understood his apprehension. I wish I had done more in my situation.

After a number of sleepless nights, Robert finally built up the courage to have a conversation with his parents to get their wills and the other estate plan documents in order.

Robert felt relieved to have all this done. It gave him peace of mind.

These documents reassured him his parents and their affairs would be handled by their loving children.

All of their important information was kept in a bright red big envelope. Everyone knew where it was kept.

His parents had named him and his two siblings as co-executors. As executors, they were equal one-third beneficiaries.

As soon as Lenora passed away from cancer, the family dynamics changed forever.

As Lenora's estate started to be settled, Sandra declared that she was entitled to more of an inheritance than her two brothers.

She produced a handwritten letter that she claimed her mother had dictated on her deathbed.

Sandra attempted to use this document to further her claim for more than the one-third of the estate she was entitled to. Her brothers objected.

As a result, Lenora's estate remained unsettled for several months.

Continuing to be dissatisfied with the equal split with her brothers, Sandra went behind their backs and tried to manipulate the estate to her benefit.

She had her father Fred, who suffered multiple ailments—including dementia, blindness, and cancer—change his will in favor of her quest for a greater share of the estate.

Her brothers only discovered this after Fred passed away a year after his wife.

The estate remains unsettled and is now before the court.

If you assume the responsibility of being an executor, and/or you become a beneficiary, be prepared to encounter human behavior at its worst.

I can attest to that after seven years, ten court appearances, and $50,000 in lawyer fees.

As an executor, you want to avoid what I call the estate triangle of conflict.

If the estate you are working to settle has at least one of these issues, any hope of the job being completed smoothly just got a whole lot more difficult.

The Estate Triangle of Conflict

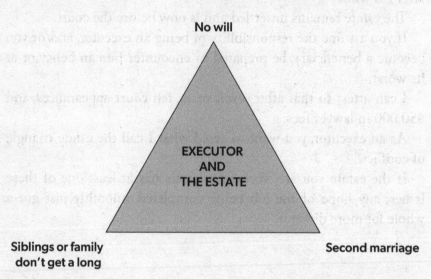

No will

EXECUTOR
AND
THE ESTATE

Siblings or family
don't get a long

Second marriage

What is an executor?

An executor (liquidator in the province of Quebec) is a person or institution appointed by a testator (a person who has made a will or bequeathed money or other valuables as part of a legacy) to carry out the terms of their will.

As an executor, you are responsible for making sure that any debts or creditors that the deceased may have incurred are paid off.

You must also ensure that a final tax return is filed on behalf of the deceased and any money owing to the government is paid in full.

Any remaining money or property is to be distributed according to the testator's wishes.

This will require a careful reading of the will and, subsequently, taking the necessary steps to ensure the distribution of the testator's remaining wealth according to their stated wishes.

Do you have to accept the role of executor? The decision is totally up to you. It's not always an easy one.

If you are chosen by a relative or a friend to be an executor, you may feel honored to fill this role, especially as this is the person's last requested favor of you.

Andrew's uncle died and his mother was executor; she refused because of her age. Andrew was the second person named in the will by his uncle.

Though they were close, being an executor brought on new responsibilities he did not expect.

Andrew told me, "I saw him all the time. We were close, but we were not close in terms of talking about his finances.

"I roughly knew which bank he dealt with. But I had to go through his paperwork and find which banks he was getting statements from, where his credit cards were from, etc."

When you're dealing with somebody like an uncle or a secondary relative, not your parents, you have to get their whole financial picture.

You may also feel that you have no choice. The relative or friend likely chose you as someone who could be trusted to carry out their last wishes.

You may have also been selected as the fairest or most diplomatic member of that person's family or community.

You may also feel that you are best able to have the estate settled with the least number of hassles in the shortest amount of time.

You also have the right to decline taking on the job of being an executor.

William's uncle was a hardworking man and did everything right. He had two children, but he did not have confidence in either of them when it came to managing finances.

The relationship between his children was always volatile. Both loved their father, but only one child went really went out of their way to look after him.

When William's uncle died, he left a small estate to the children, to be split 50/50.

One day, William got a phone call from a lawyer informing him that he had been designated as executor to his uncle's estate.

As much as he loved his uncle, he declined.

William said to the lawyer, "You have to accept my resignation, and you have to cc me on the letter, because I need everybody involved with the estate to know, legally, that I'm declining because I was not aware that I was put as executor."

So, the lawyer sent a letter to his two cousins, including William. He declined being the executor because, as he put it, "I did not want to be part of this 'shit show.'"

Later in the book, in the section on how to pick an executor, you will find out about the "shit show" William refused to be a part of.

The choice is yours. You can always decline to be an executor and pass the responsibility onto someone else.

Before you make the decision, ask yourself:

- Do I want to do this? Or do I feel that I must do this out of a sense of family obligation or friendship?

- Is it in the best interests of the people I love and myself to assume this responsibility? Would it be better to leave this to someone else?
- Am I up to the task?

Here are some questions to ask yourself if you would make a good executor:

Are you honest?
- Do you have a lot of patience?
- Are you well organized?
- Do you pay attention to details?
- Can you get along with other people?
- Do you have time to spare?
- Can you take time off from work during the day?
- Are you willing to take time off from work during the day?

Settling an estate can take six months to a year, and in some cases, even longer. It took me seven years.

You will need to dedicate a number of hours (more than 100) on and off to overseeing everything to its necessary completion.

Deciding whether to accept the responsibility of being an executor may be difficult if you do not have one or more of the above-mentioned elements.

However, you should not be frightened away from this responsibility by a lack of related expertise—legal or financial.

Professional assistance is always available through an accountant, financial adviser, real estate agent, and/or lawyer, with their payment typically made with some of the estate's funds.

So it will not be coming out of your pocket.

Make no mistake about it. If you want to settle the estate as efficiently as you can, you are going to need a team of professionals.

The right professionals can help you, as the executor, and the other beneficiaries stay on track with a realistic and efficient timeline.

Even with a professional to help out, each estate and every family dynamic is unique.

Chances are things may not go as smoothly as you would think or like.

Therefore, if you decide to assume the responsibility of an executor, go into the process with your eyes wide open.

Grace was an executor of her mother's estate, and she remembers it involved a lot of accounting.

She said, "You have to pay all the bills. Be comfortable dealing with banks, dealing with lawyers. You're going to be in charge of the funeral. You're going to be doing all that stuff, and you need to have the time to do it."

Don't be worried by how family members or the other beneficiaries will react to you taking charge, or by their surprise or dissatisfaction with some aspect of the estate's settlement.

From what I've experienced and have heard from clients, I firmly believe that every estate has a story that goes with it.

Long-festering, often deep-rooted family conflicts usually surface that may or may not have been apparent when the deceased was still alive.

As an executor, you need to have a bit of a thick skin because we're talking about money, and money is important to a lot of people.

As an executor, you have to be prepared to answer questions about your conduct, and if you're not willing to do it—if you're going to get your back up and say, "Oh, you're accusing me of being a thief"—then you need to re-think if you want to do the job.

You can always say no.

The Executor Help Solution

The biggest dangers and problems that cause stress:

- Make sure you are up to doing the job.
- Do not be afraid to ask for help.
- Communicate with beneficiaries on a regular basis.

What you need to do to get started:

- Locate and review will.
- Notify the beneficiaries of the death, if necessary, and advise them of their entitlement under the will.
- Assist with funeral arrangements and placement of an obituary.
- Obtain multiple copies of the certified certificate of death from the funeral director (at least fifteen).
- Arrange for care of any pets.
- Cancel all credit cards, memberships, passport, driver's license, health insurance card, and social insurance number or social security number.
- Cancel telephone and cable, if residence is vacant.
- Redirect mail and cancel any subscriptions.

How this helps you:

- Now you will have a starting point.

For an executor checklist, go to www.davidedey.com/resources

5 problems you create by not having a good estate plan

1. Your survivors will pay too much in taxes.
2. Your survivors will waste time and money in court (including attorney fees).
3. Your current will is outdated and no longer represents what you want.
4. Your will is old and you don't remember what it says. Your circumstances have changed over the years. So should your will.
5. Your family will break up and never be the same again.

Chapter 4
What you need to know to be an executor

Jerry Garcia of the rock group Grateful Dead died of a heart attack on August 9, 1995, at the age of 53.

Not a fan of the music, but do enjoy the Ben and Jerry ice cream flavor Cherry Garcia.

In any case.

He had a will, but that was not enough, as the estate ended up spending a lot of time in court.

What it also had was an element from the triangle of conflict: a second marriage.

Several lawsuits involving the estate continued on for about thirteen years!

Jerry's executor was his third wife, Deborah Koons Garcia.

As with any executor who is left to settle an estate that is a mess (and includes an ingredient from the triangle of conflict), it took a lot of time to clean it up.

She was quoted as saying it became like a job.

The estate was worth about $15 million, and within months of his death, she was facing claims estimated at $50 million!

One of the largest claims was made by Garcia's second wife, Carolyn Adams, who claimed that Garcia had agreed to pay her $5 million for support at the rate of $250,000 per year.

She and Garcia had made up their own one-page separation agreement, without legal advice.

Garcia signed the agreement approximately eighteen months before his death so he could get a divorce and marry Deborah.

The problem was that the estate did not have that kind of cash to settle with Carolyn.

Carolyn took the estate to court and won.

Deborah appealed, and the parties eventually settled for about $1.2 million.

A claim was also made by one of Garcia's daughters, Keelan Garcia, who felt she wasn't left enough in the will. She settled with the estate in 2008 for undisclosed cash and an interest in the Cherry Garcia trademark.

One of the most interesting claims involved Garcia's guitar maker, Doug Erwin.

He was the only non-family member named in the will. Garcia left his four guitars to him.

However, Garcia's band members in the Grateful Dead claimed that the guitars belonged to the band and not to Garcia, personally. Erwin sued and settled for two of the guitars.

At auction, the guitars fetched almost $1.8 million! Erwin then tried to get the estate to pay the taxes arising from the sale.

He failed at that.

Deborah Koons Garcia turned out to be a pretty astute executor.

She was able to pare $50 million of claims down to $700,000, according to the 2003 documentary *Can't Take It with You*.

As executor, the responsibility of making sure taxes and outstanding debts are paid before settling the estate lies with you.

To make certain that you don't have any trouble with creditors and beneficiaries, you must always remember to:

1. keep accurate financial records of all estate-related transactions.
2. know what money is owed and to whom.
3. make copies of all estate-related and -settling receipts.

4. keep a detailed log of all the time you spend administering the estate.
5. keep a detailed log of any travel for the estate (including exact kilometers).

It is essential to keep these, along with any other documents, organized to satisfy the beneficiaries and/or a court, should any dispute arise.

Depending on the people and matters involved, an average estate can take from six months to a year to be settled—even longer if an executor or a co-executor delays completing their duties or if the estate is complicated.

It is not uncommon for many beneficiaries to be unaware of the work and time required to settle an estate.

Beneficiaries have no problem taking an executor to court if they feel that the estate is not being handled properly or is taking too long to settle.

Even if beneficiaries do become impatient, it is wisest to wait until you have received a tax clearance certificate from the CRA to protect yourself and them. Be sure to get a judgment from the probate court, in the US, before distributing all the estate's assets.

The clearance certificate or probate judgment confirms that the deceased's tax affairs are in order and paid in full.

If you distribute any funds or property to beneficiaries prior to getting the okay from the government or courts, you, as the executor, can be personally liable for any of the estate's still-unpaid taxes.

That's not to say that as the executor, you cannot make any distributions before receiving the certificate. You can make inheritance distributions.

However, it is wise to consult a lawyer to determine whether it would be a good idea for the beneficiaries to sign a release form before handing out any distributions.

The other smart thing to do is talk with your accountant to make sure there is enough money to pay the taxes and the outstanding bills.

As the executor, you might personally be responsible for any mistakes you make while administering the estate.

If there's any financial loss to the estate, you as the executor may have to repay that loss out of your own pocket.

When do an executor's duties begin?

The executor's duties start before the will is probated.

The executor's job is to begin preserving the estate immediately after the death of the person.

The Executor Help Solution

The biggest dangers and problems that cause stress:

- An unorganized estate.
- An ingredient from the triangle of conflict.
- Dealing with creditors.
- Spending a lot of your time on settling the estate.

What you need to do and where to get the help:

- Don't be surprised by beneficiaries and their actions.
- Have a lawyer as part of your team.
- Be prepared for unexpected claims against the estate and have a plan to deal with them.

How this helps you:

- You have a plan to deal with creditors.
- You won't pay out money until outstanding issues are settled.
- You will be able to sleep at night.

Chapter 5
Administrative duties, handling an estate

Vincent was asked to be executor for his dying brother, Carson.

He was honored to be asked and wanted to follow his brother's wishes.

Carson had a daughter and sole beneficiary, Makayla. She did not grow up knowing her father, but later in life, they began to forge a relationship.

She loved her uncle Vincent and was glad he was a shoulder to lean on during this difficult time.

As the family started to meet at the hospital, in between visits, Vincent would often go to his brother's apartment. He told everyone he was going "to pick up some things."

Carson loved cars and had a vintage Mustang, which was his most prized automobile.

When Carson died, Makayla received her "inheritance," and Vincent hired cleaners to go in and clean the apartment. In his mind, the estate was closed.

Remember how happy Vincent was to be his brother's executor?

Here's the rest of the story, which demonstrates why it is so important that if you accept to be an executor, you must complete the job to the best of your ability.

For some reason, Carson didn't believe in the banking system or banks.

All the family knew about the huge amount of money stashed in the small apartment in which he lived for over thirty years.

As family gathered at the hospital to say their final goodbyes, a lawyer and family friend showed up with the will and gave it to Vincent, the executor.

Carson's wishes were that all assets were to be left to Makayla. He left nothing to his siblings.

Apart from his assets in Canada, he owned real estate in the Caribbean. It was his wish that Makayla inherit this as well.

A few other specific items, such as a vintage car, were to be left to a nephew.

This did not sit well with Vincent, though he assured everyone he was comfortable with the wishes of his brother.

He did initially carry out his duties.

He made the funeral arrangements, but his actions showed he did not care how the money was spent.

When the final bill came in for the funeral, it was in the neighborhood of $50,000.

The family was horrified, as he was clearly burning through the estate's money.

Vincent never did a statement of holdings, and to this day, Makayla still does not know how much money was in the house.

Everyone wondered, what happened to Carson's prized Mustang? If it was sold, where's the money?

Vincent took more than two years to file the tax return and pay the back taxes.

As for the real estate in the Caribbean, that still has not been settled, six years after Carson's death.

After repeated requests from Makayla and other family members to resign as executor, Vincent finally did.

Makayla no longer has a relationship with Vincent.

To properly administer an estate as a trustee, you must act in the best interests of the beneficiaries of the estate.

Be transparent and efficient to get all the related matters concluded as soon as possible.

This requires you to promptly fill out all of the necessary forms and complete all the necessary government filings.

Make sure not to put yourself in jeopardy in any way, so you don't become liable in the future.

Keep a dated record of all your actions on behalf of the estate or estate trust, so you can relate these details to the beneficiaries, if they ever ask.

It is often really wise to obtain advice from one or more professionals familiar with the settling of estates, such as a lawyer, accountant, realtor, and/or financial adviser.

Professionals will tell you if something is outside their realm of expertise and put you in contact with the proper consultant for a particular situation.

Of course, you may not have to hire all of these experts. It really depends on the size and difficulty of the estate.

It should be your goal, as the executor, to conclude all your duties within a year at most.

This will require you to do all of the following:

1. Follow the will as it is written.
2. Work in the best interests of the beneficiaries.
3. Show no favoritism toward any beneficiaries.
4. Share any relevant important information with the beneficiaries, tax authorities, creditors, etc.
5. Keep a record of all your actions on behalf of the estate.
6. Pay all outstanding bills.
7. File a final tax return and pay any owing amount from the estate.
8. Sometimes you may have to pay any legitimate expenses for the estate's management out of your own pocket as the executor. (Be sure to keep receipts to be reimbursed by the estate.) Pay any professionals who helped you settle the estate.
9. In Canada, once you receive the government's tax clearance certificate, distribute the estate's assets in accordance with the will.

In the United States, the probate court provides the final

ruling on division and distribution of assets to beneficiaries, once taxes and other debts have been paid.

In order to officially close an estate in the United States, you'll need to work with a probate court to finalize the process.

Don't try to make the will fairer than it seems, as this could lead to you being sued.

Mediator and estate litigation lawyer Charles Ticker, in his book *Bobby Gets Bubkes*, writes that equal is not always fair.

Don't be fooled into thinking that dividing an estate equally between siblings will solve the issue of fairness.

He says siblings who want to fight or who have long-standing differences will often find a way to fight over an estate.

There are many reported cases where a sibling is not happy with an equal division of the estate because the parent, before they died, had promised to give that sibling a particular asset or gift.

As executor, you will find out if the will needs to be probated.

What is probate?

It is the process to prove a will is valid. You need to consult a lawyer if this needs to be done.

The process will verify that no other document was written before this will.

The probate will also confirm that the will is indeed legitimate as the deceased's final instructions for the estate, and was prepared by the deceased while they were of sound mind and without any undue pressure by any other individual.

A lawyer will map out the steps to be completed. Every province in Canada and every state in the United States has its own set of rules. This is why it's usually so important to have a lawyer as part of your advisory team.

The Executor Help Solution

The biggest dangers, problems that cause stress and court cases:

- You don't follow the wishes in the will of the deceased.
- You don't communicate with beneficiaries.
- You don't share all relevant information with the beneficiaries, tax authorities, creditors, agents, and relevant third parties.
- You don't keep a dated record of all your actions on behalf of the estate.
- You don't pay all of the deceased's outstanding bills.
- You don't file a final tax report on behalf of the deceased and pay any owing amount from the estate.
- You don't get final written acknowledgment from the government that the estate is closed.

What you need to do and where to get the help:

- Carry out the wishes of the deceased exactly.
- Stay in touch with beneficiaries on a regular basis so they know what is going on.
- Keep records of everything you do and get help from your accountant.
- Work with an accountant to file tax returns and resolve any other tax issues.

How this helps you:

- You can show you have been transparent with everything.
- You are avoiding potential fights with beneficiaries.
- You will feel confident because you are organized.

How to pick the right guardian

Parents with minor children should agree on what they are looking for in a guardian named in their wills.
  This could include:

- ✓ Their willingness to be a guardian.
- ✓ Their financial situation.
- ✓ Where the child might live.
- ✓ Their values, religion, or political beliefs.
- ✓ Their skills as a parent.
- ✓ Their age and health.

Chapter 6
Secrets to successful co-executor existence

Peter, Steven, and Marie were designated co-executors of their father's estate, even though the three never really got along as children or adults.

Peter did not expect anything to change when it came to the estate's settlement, as he always found that Marie acted selfishly, always putting her interests unfairly ahead of what might be fair to her brothers.

Steven always found himself in the middle of Marie and Peter's arguments, but still had a soft spot for his sister.

He continued to be willing to give her a chance to do the right things after their father's death, but would not be surprised if she tried to obtain more than her share of the estate.

He also knew to expect conflicts between Marie and Peter.

Since the estate was left equally to all three, it was in their best interests to get it settled as soon as possible so they could resume their lives.

After talking to friends who had been executors, Peter realized it would be best if he withdrew from his role as one of the executors.

He knew it would be difficult to put his resentments toward his sister aside.

Things would likely go smoother if Steven and Marie, who got along better, were the only co-executors.

Steven assured his brother that he would keep him informed about the progress being made toward the estate's settlement, as well as anything that required settling a difference of opinion between Marie and him.

It was also decided that more than one signature would be required to sign any checks on the estate's behalf, so that no one was acting solely on their own.

As a result, the estate was settled faster and with less stress than it might have been if all three had stayed involved as co-executors.

Every family is different and so is every estate.

Some have a sole executor to settle the estate, while others have more than one executor—even several—named.

Co-executors are often named if there are two or more children in a family and a parent does not want to favor one child over the other.

Is this a good idea?

Being a co-executor can turn out to be a blessing, or a nightmare. It all depends on who is involved and how things are handled.

The tasks involved do not differ from settling the estate alone. So, it will depend on the people involved to determine whether this will be a generally pleasant and more efficient process or sheer hell.

You and your co-executors must work collaboratively.

Even if you divvy up tasks, both co-executors (or at least two of them, if there are more) will be required to sign checks on behalf of the estate.

This could pose a problem if co-executors live far apart or don't agree on matters.

It's not uncommon that one executor makes a decision about the estate without consulting the other(s).

The result is often a court battle, with one or more of the executors asking for another to be removed from the process.

If you want to save time, energy, frustration, and money, put any petty feelings you may have about the other co-executor(s) aside.

It does not matter who might be at fault for an issue, even if it's clearly some kind of tantrum or silly matter.

You need to be the adult.

Your number one priority is to correctly settle the estate as quickly as possible.

Courts do not like to get involved in estate issues. If a dispute erupts between a co-executor and you that can only be resolved by legal means, it could end up costing each of you dearly.

Try your best to resolve any differences of opinion amicably.

When I met Grace, she talked about her mother, who died and left behind rental properties, cash, and investment accounts to all of her three daughters in equal amounts.

Grace was one of the three co-executors with her sisters.

Her younger sister immediately joined with the other sister to start controlling the mother's assets.

Grace tried to get co-operation so she could do an inventory of the mother's belongings, but the younger sister refused to help and suggested keeping the mother's home and renovating it so she could live in it. She also wanted to keep all the house possessions (which were mostly of sentimental value).

Grace did not want to take her sisters to court.

You always want to find ways to avoid going to court.

Be prepared to be tested mentally, physically and emotionally.

I had to be in court or be represented by my lawyer over ten times.

I also did not realize how much of a toll it was taking on my life. Throughout 2017, it was a non-stop battle. The other side did everything they could to delay the process every step of the way.

On a typical cold and gray day in November, I was not feeling well, and just as a precaution, I went to the hospital.

Two hours later, the doctors told me I needed to have double bypass heart surgery.

Clearly, the stress of having to deal with the nonsense of settling the estate that had taken more than six years to that point had caught up to me.

Susan says I always keep my stress inside. As usual, she is right.

I thought to myself, *No problem. I just need to get better in time to be back in court in January.*

Probably not the best strategy.

Once you decide you have to go to court, your emotions also take over. You really do not think straight.

I wanted my day in court. Surely the judge would see how unreasonable and difficult the other party was.

Turns out that "day in court" is never just a day.

Trials can go on for several days or weeks. In our case, it took seven years.

Luckily, I did not have to be in court in January as it got postponed to a later date, which made Susan and my sister Velma happy and relieved.

According to conflict expert Kirstin Lund, when someone is refusing to come to the table, it can often be because they're happy or satisfied with the status quo.

In this case, Grace's sisters' belief that they have controlling interest of the assets could be a reason they are refusing to be co-operative.

The sisters may need another reason to come to the table. But before anyone gets served with court papers.

Grace can try a few things.

She needs to find a way to remind her sisters of their personal connection.

One strategy to improve their relationship could be to invite the sisters out for lunch or do something that isn't just about the estate.

Maybe it's just about asking:

- How are you doing?
- How can we work together?
- Is there anything I can do to help?

When trust breaks down, we make negative assumptions about the other person's motivation, and it can snowball to a place where we villainize people.

This is where these sisters are at, and if Grace invites them out to lunch, they most likely will be very skeptical and question her motives.

"Is she trying to suck up to us so we'll do what she wants? Or is she just trying to get something from Mom's estate?"

This may or may not be the right strategy for these sisters, though it could be the first step in trying to change the status quo.

From what I've seen over the years with clients, this kind of conflict can be traced to problems the siblings had with one another when they were children.

It is not uncommon for adult siblings to refer to negative childhood episodes, even though what happened when they were kids has nothing to do with potential lawsuits or settling of the estate.

I thought, like Grace, that if siblings are treated equally under the terms of a parent's will, then there would be no reason for an estate fight.

Or a dispute could be due to a second marriage.

Rocker Tom Petty's widow and his two daughters finally came to an agreement two years after he died, deciding to work as equals in the release of additional recordings and other projects.

Dana York Petty, the singer's widow, and daughters Adria and Anakin Violette, from his first marriage, had been at odds in the months after his death at 66 on October 2, 2017, just a week after he and the Heartbreakers completed a triumphant, six-month fortieth-anniversary world tour.

Differences emerged following the rollout of "Tom Petty: An American Treasure" and "Tom Petty and the Heartbreakers: The Best of Everything" and led to a $5-million lawsuit filed by his daughters against their stepmother, who countersued.

The daughters argued that their father wanted all three parties equally involved in decision-making regarding his estate, and Dana Petty countered that he had made her sole executor.

Part of their joint statement said they resolved their differences and dismissed all litigation matters that had been filed related to Tom's estate.

Each of them sincerely regretted that in their intense grief over Tom's tragic death, actions were taken that were hurtful to one another.

It also specified:

Each member of the family will have equal standing
in Tom Petty Legacy LLC and will work together
on all future endeavors."
The business will build upon Tom's forty-plus years
of great music and his historic career.

What could be fairer than being treated equally?

Before you decide to head to court, whether you are an executor
or beneficiary, why not try mediation? It could be your last chance to
come to an agreement.

One of the main advantages of mediation is it saves everybody
a lot of court costs. Mediation, particularly when it involves estate
disputes, can be very successful in getting matters settled. Another
big advantage of mediation is that it's private.

The Executor Help Solution

The biggest dangers and problems that cause stress:

- Dealing with difficult co-executors.
- Making negative childhood episodes an issue today.
- The threat of going to court.

What you need to do to get started:

- Find some common ground so you can communicate and continue settling the estate.
- Look to speak with a mediator.
- As a last resort, talk to your lawyer.

How this helps you:

- Saves thousands of dollars in lawyer fees.

7 Questions answered for when dealing with beneficiaries

How can a beneficiary challenge the executor of a will?

1. If a demand letter by an attorney does not produce a result, there is a legal proceeding that allows the court to legally remove the executor who fails in their duties to liquidate the estate in a proper and diligent manner

How can a beneficiary get a copy of a will?

2. The executor has a legal obligation to disclose the will to all heirs who write a demand letter from a lawyer

How to change the beneficiary of a will?

3. As executor, you can't change the will. Only the testator can. They can make a codicil to change a beneficiary, which is a modification to the will, or preferably simply draft a new will

How to notify a beneficiary of a will?

4. Notification of beneficiary can be communicated by any reasonable practical means, but do so in writing in order to have proof of this notification (e.g., email).

How to pay a beneficiary of a will?

5. Payment is made by a check from the estate account. Always obtain a receipt acknowledging payment of the legacy. if it is real estate (i.e., an immoveable), you will require a notary to draft a declaration of transmission of the property

What happens if a beneficiary of a will dies?

6. If the beneficiary dies after the testator, but prior to payment of the legacy the majority of wills provide for an alternate heir (or legatee). If none is provided, the court determines the beneficiary

What happens if a beneficiary of a will dies before the testator?

7. If the beneficiary predeceases the testator, then a new will should promptly be drafted

Chapter 7
How to deal effectively with beneficiaries

In researching this book, I came across a surprising story that shocked and saddened me.

It involved the estate of Nelson Mandela. Here was a man who lived his life to bring peace and be a global advocate for human rights.

I was fortunate to see him live and hear him speak when he visited Montreal and the Union United Church on June 19, 1990.

That day, security was tight inside and outside the church.

If you were one of the fortunate few hundred inside the packed church, you were not allowed to leave.

I can still hear the roar of the crowd outside vibrate inside as his motorcade got closer.

It was magical when he walked into the church with the choir singing (my dad, with his deep bass voice, was in the choir—that was so cool!) an up-lifting gospel song, and there he was, dancing down the aisle to the podium.

There he was, the man I had only read about and watched on TV —a man who had changed the world.

Years later, on a trip to South Africa for Susan's birthday, one of our excursions had us take a boat to Robben Island to the prison where he spent twenty-seven years.

(Side note: If you ever want to visit a beautiful country, go to South Africa. Experience everything—the people, the food, and the safaris. It was the best trip of my life.)

I could not believe how small Nelson Mandela's cell was and how he and the other prisoners had to carry a bucket around as their toilet everywhere they went.

If they were lucky to shower, it was in a small, crammed room where only ten to twelve people could fit in at one time. How he managed to last all those years in those inhumane conditions made me admire and appreciate him even more for what he was willing to give up for his beliefs and to help others.

He never gave up fighting to free his country from racial division, and he led an essentially peaceful revolution, which led to his release from prison in 1990.

And you would think, for everything this man did for his people and the world, his values would be passed on down to his family.

No. His family members acted like many other families who have individuals who always think of themselves first.

Author Cindy Arledge calls it, in her book by the same title, the *Cur$e of Inheritance*.

The cur$e of inheritance is an ugly monster of jealousy, fear, and selfishness that crushes families, eats money, and destroys lives.

She says the cur$e of inheritance is born in an environment of loss and grief by unprepared heirs who feel entitled to unearned wealth and forget to see each other as human beings.

Mandela's children and grandchildren began fighting, even before he died in 2013.

Mandela's eldest grandson, Mandla Mandela, was accused of shady maneuvering, hoping to make Nelson's gravesite into a profitable tourist attraction.

Many of his heirs have tried to profit from his name and image. Two granddaughters started a reality show called *Being Mandela*.

Others started a House of Mandela wine label. And then there's the company hawking fashion accessories and t-shirts.

There are press reports that dozens of companies already use the Mandela name in Africa, while his tribal name, Madiba, is in use by more than 140 companies.

Many of his family members feel it is their turn to profit.

As Reuters reported, one of his granddaughters said: "If everybody wants a little bit of the Madiba magic, why is it so sacrilegious for the rightful owners ... to use the Madiba magic?"

Whatever your reason for agreeing to be an executor—whether out of a sense of duty or honor—this is likely the one and only time in your life that you will be called upon to do such a thankless job.

Why thankless? If all goes well, it will be seen by the beneficiaries as having been no big deal for you to do.

If it doesn't, you'll likely be targeted for some or all of their discontentment, possibly even resentment.

As to why only the one time ... Executors are typically a very personal choice that a deceased makes, putting their trust in that person or people to properly and fairly settle their estate.

This is not something that we're routinely called upon to do because most of us don't have the professional training.

Dealing with lawyers, accountants, real estate agents, and financial advisers all takes a lot of time and effort.

There's a lot of paperwork involved. So there has to be strong motivation to agree to do all this.

Plus, there are the beneficiaries. They could be wonderful, or they could soon have you asking why you ever agreed to all this estate grief.

Who is a beneficiary?

A beneficiary is an individual who has been designated by a will to receive something of value from the estate.

It might be a sum of money, real estate, land, or a particular item, such as a piece of jewelry or a work of art.

Beneficiaries can make your life easy or become your biggest nightmare.

The beneficiaries who are reasonable people and in no big hurry to obtain their inheritance only need to be kept informed regularly by you as to how the estate's settlement is progressing.

You could keep these beneficiaries up to date through an email, teleconferencing session, or online virtual meeting every one or two weeks.

The key is to communicate. If reasonable people are made aware of the steps and the realistic timing for their completion, they will likely be more patient with the process.

Any unforeseen delays or circumstances should be promptly related so that they can adjust their expectations.

While clear communications may seem to be a simple process, you need to be prepared to deal with a difficult beneficiary.

Too often, there are people who are unrealistically impatient with the process, angered that they weren't put in charge of the estate, believe they are entitled to more than what's been designated to them, and willing to be manipulative in an attempt to gain a bigger share or property or an item they deem should belong only to them.

Some people are naturally difficult, even argumentative, no matter what.

You must always be prepared for anything. It's amazing how people change—show a totally different side of themselves—when there is an inheritance.

Many want their inheritance as soon as possible. They are not interested in the process you must follow to settle the estate.

As mentioned, some feel they should be entitled to more than what has been designated to them.

While we're usually talking about money, it could also be items of monetary and/or sentimental value.

It could be there's this one lava lamp designated to no one in particular in the will but wanted by several of the deceased's relatives, and it disappears from the estate home after one of the beneficiaries visits.

So, what do you do in such a case?

The difficult and entitled beneficiary is the most likely person to want to take you to court.

Sometimes you can call a person's bluff, or find a resolution that avoids legal action.

However, you should never be surprised at the lengths some people will go when it comes to an inheritance.

Don't forget: some people might have been waiting for years for an inheritance to solve their monetary and other woes, regardless of whether the estate may have never held this promise for them.

So how to deal with difficult beneficiaries?

1. Make it clear that you will be following the will's instructions exactly as written.
2. 2. Emphasize that you cannot possibly change any aspects of the will even if you thought doing so would make the estate's settlement fairer to everyone because that could expose you to a potential lawsuit.
3. Let them know that it is your goal to settle the estate within one year.
4. State at the outset (and confirm same in a written letter or email) that you will not under any circumstance pay out any money from the estate until all of the deceased's taxes have been paid and you have received tax clearance certification from the Canadian government.
   In the US, you will not pay out any money until you have gotten a judgment from the probate court.
5. Let them know you will be keeping them informed every week to two weeks, either by email, a scheduled teleconference, or virtual online meeting.
6. Let them know you will not allow any personal or household items to be taken before the estate is settled or given to anyone who is not named in the will.
7. Some ways to resolve a fight between two beneficiaries if they both want the same item is to flip a coin or have a vote by all the beneficiaries. If you can't get an agreement, suggest putting

the item up for sale with the profits equally divided among all of the beneficiaries.

8. If the will says the inheritance for certain beneficiaries, such as minors, has to be put in a trust, explain that a trust will be set up according to the will's directions. Make it clear the trust will be established according to the law. Make them understand this no matter how much the beneficiary or relatives, life partners, or friends disagree or would like it to be set up differently.

9. Make it clear as executor you are under no obligation to share the contents of the will with the beneficiaries. As executor, you are only required to let each beneficiary know that they are named in the will and what they have been designated by the will to receive from the estate. Explain that once the will is probated (if this is necessary, which it likely will be in a contentious environment), it becomes a public document that you can share at that time or that a beneficiary can obtain directly from a court registry.

Providing all the details of the will to everyone runs the risk of giving anyone who feels slighted or entitled to additional funds or items of value the motivation to object to the estate's planned settlement.

And the last thing you want is to give an individual any reason to slow down the process and even possibly go to court to have you removed as the executor.

If you do encounter a difficult beneficiary, there are a number of strategies to deal with the situation as effectively and efficiently as possible.

First off, don't take any offensive comments personally. It is amazing how often another unpleasant—at times even ugly—side of people emerges when an inheritance is at stake.

You may hardly recognize this new character in siblings or other family members.

Understand they are suffering from the cur$e of inheritance.

It truly is amazing how often an inheritance—even one of a modest value—brings out the selfishness and greed of relatives.

A lot of people believe they are entitled to a greater share than designated to them.

Or they immediately demand their share, revealing that they have been waiting for years for the parent or other relation to die to claim this inheritance and remedy their own financial situation.

Personal relationships, especially family dynamics, are often changed forever, with an estate dispute often resulting in the breakup of a family.

In many cases, the fallout is permanent, with certain family members never speaking again.

Your responsibilities are limited to having the estate properly settled as quickly as possible, keeping the beneficiaries informed from the outset about what each is entitled to receive, and providing updates every week or two about your progress in concluding the estate's affairs.

The Executor Help Solution

The biggest dangers and problems that cause stress:

- Be prepared to deal with beneficiaries who have the cur$e of inheritance.
- Listening to beneficiaries and not doing what you have to do to settle the estate.
- Being surprised by the behavior of people you thought you knew.

What you need to do and where to get the help:

- Don't listen to people who are not beneficiaries (spouses of beneficiaries, cousins, non-family members).
- Don't take any shortcuts to settle the estate in order to please beneficiaries, as this will open you to being sued.
- Stay transparent with everything you do with the help of your accountant, lawyer and financial adviser.

How this helps you:

- You will be prepared to handle beneficiary conflicts as best you can be.
- You are taking the steps not to invite lawsuits.
- You are being honest and transparent.
- For more on the rights of beneficiaries, go to www.davidedey. com/resources

4 Ideas you could try to fix your broken sibling relationship, or not!

All too often, family members cut each other off due to disagreements over their parents' estates, in-law conflicts, or hurt feelings.

Here are some ways you may want to consider if you have any interest in salvaging your relationship

Reconcile:

Just because you reconcile doesn't mean you have to forgive and forget. How much effort are you willing to put in?

Accept the family member for who they are:

If you have a sibling or a family member who is not sensitive or self-aware, you need to make the decision. Are you willing to accept it and move forward?

Accept there are some relationships where you will never be close:

You may just decide, for whatever reason, you will just never have a relationship and it is best to move on with your life.

Or you can just let it go

Holding on to anger, hurt, or disappointment is bad for your mind and body. (Believe me, I know.) The best thing to do is just move on with your life. Make the decision to finally put the sibling(s) or family members in your rearview mirror.

Chapter 8
The digital world

Four years after the death of her husband of forty-one years, Carol Anne found herself in a battle with Apple.

She was the executor and sole beneficiary of her husband's estate.

She wanted access to an Apple account she shared with her husband but which was under his name.

It was to fulfill a promise she made to him before he died.

But instead of giving her the password she had forgotten, the tech giant created obstacles that resulted in expensive legal costs.

It seems they wanted an order from the court to give her access.

Tech companies refusing to hand over digital assets can be a problem for executors.

This can affect everything from stocks, insurance policies, and PayPal, to gaming credits, social media posts, and family photos.

As people's online presence becomes more widespread, digital assets become another crucial responsibility of the executor.

What are digital assets?

It is an electronic record in which an individual has a right or interest.

What are considered to be digital assets?

- Personal email
- Communication
- Social media

- Other online accounts
- Electronic files
- Photos
- Videos
- Applications
- Information stored on physical devices
- Money-management
- Financial accounts
- Digital assets related to a business

As an executor, you have to be aware of criminals who will often target the deceased.

It's an opportunity for theft and fraud. For example, passcodes, such as a mother's maiden name, may actually be printed in the obituary in the local newspaper.

For those without a conscience, it may be too easy to resist.

The most common method of committing online fraud is for the criminal to obtain sufficient information so they are able to impersonate the deceased.

Even if the person is deceased, as long as accounts are active, there is nothing to prevent them from withdrawing funds, making purchases, and even placing substantial mortgages against property.

If you are the executor, you need to know where all the information related to all digital assets is kept.

You need to shut them down.

You must also figure out how to deal with the deceased individual's social media accounts.

When doing this, you may wonder:

- How can you delete or freeze an online account when someone passes away?
- What is the safest option to deal with a deceased person's social media accounts?

Options vary with all social media brands and online profiles regarding what happens to the account when someone dies.

It is up to the executor to decide what to do, if anything. Sometimes, memorializing is the desired action; however, deleting the account may be best in other cases.

Each website and company has unique terms of service (TOS).

It can be overwhelming to get through and decipher all this information, so it is best to take time to read all the information found here and decide what strategy to take when it comes to a deceased person's social media accounts.

Options for Controlling and Handling Social Media Accounts of a Deceased Person

You have three options for handling social media accounts. These include:

1. Memorialize

With this option, the profile settings remain as they were when a person died. While it depends on the settings, it may be possible for others to leave messages on the deceased person's page.

2. Deactivate

With this option, the profile, comments, likes, and photos are hidden until the executor (or a family member) reactivates it. With this option, neither the information nor content is destroyed.

3. Delete

Deleting the account means that all comments, photos, and the entire profile are permanently erased. No one will be able to see any information that was once contained in the account.

The Existence of a Deceased Person's Social Media Account After Death

Until the social media company where a deceased person had an account is notified of their death, the account will remain in place and active.

Every platform has unique practices and policies regarding how an account can be controlled or managed after a person's death.

Some social media sites will allow a person's profile to be memorialized.

When this is done, the word "remembering" is put ahead of the person's name, and it will not appear in "people you may know" sections, send out reminders for the person's birthday, or show up in Facebook ads.

If the executor is named as the account's legal contact, this is the individual who can manage and monitor the account when it is memorialized.

If there is no legacy contact selected, the executor must prove they have the right to take control of the account.

This should be provided by the documentation provided when the individual was named as the executor of the estate.

Why Deleting the Account May be Necessary

After someone dies, there is the possibility that news reporters will "snoop" around, trying to find a story or to get a comment. Also, insurance companies may use the information to refuse the payout on a life insurance policy.

While this may seem far-fetched, it is something that has happened and could happen again.

In many cases, simply deleting these accounts is the best course of action.

Google

A single Google account may be linked to an array of different products, which include YouTube, Gmail, and Google Drive (to name a few).

Before moving forward with deleting this account, it is necessary to ensure it is not linked to the deceased person's spouse, as this may impact their ability to access certain information or files.

If necessary, it is possible to export the data before deleting the account.

This is essentially a copy or backup of the information. After the information is downloaded, the account can be deleted.

You can follow the instructions provided by the information on the Google account support page.

Facebook

With Facebook, you can memorialize, deactivate, or delete the account. To delete the account, it is necessary to follow the instructions provided on Facebook's website.

Facebook also requires a copy of the person's death certificate.

It is important to remember that if you delete the account, friends of the deceased person can still access the messaging history that is not stored in the actual account.

It is also possible to memorialize the account (as mentioned above).

With this option, family and friends can continue to share memories. Facebook also provides information and resources on how to memorialize the account

Another option is to create a Tribute account on Facebook.

This expands the memorialized account by letting family and friends share posts while mainlining the original timeline on the account.

There is a separate tab for Tributes, which allows people to share stories that remain separate from the account history.

Instagram

Facebook owns Instagram. This means the options for dealing with a deceased person's account are like the ones mentioned above.

You can learn to memorialize the account on Instagram's page or figure out how to delete it completely.

Amazon

There are two membership options available through Amazon. One option is a basic account, and the other is Prime membership.

With the Prime account, a fee is charged for the service. Therefore, it is necessary to close this one first. To cancel this membership, the process is simple and straightforward.

All you have to do is choose "end membership," and then all unused benefits will be refunded.

For a basic membership, you can delete the account, eliminating all linked services, such as the purchase history, photos, and anything found on Amazon drive.

However, before canceling the account, be sure to download the content you plan to save.

If you want to keep the Amazon account, change the email address to remove the payment in place or change the account settings.

Twitter

This social media platform will work with you to help deactivate the deceased person's account..

However, they do not provide full access to the account because of the privacy policy they have in place.

You can contact Twitter to discuss the necessary steps to deactivate the account.

After you have answered a few questions, Twitter will provide you with an email, providing additional instructions about what to do and how to move forward with the process.

LinkedIn

With LinkedIn, you can remove a person's profile from the platform.

There is an entire list of information that LinkedIn requires before they move forward with your request.

You must provide information like your role in the deceased person's estate or a copy of their death certificate.

Once you have the information requested, you can close the account or remove their profile by filling out a form.

Digital assets have the potential to be among the most challenging issues you may face as an executor.

You need to have a list of all accounts and their logins. By deleting them, you reduce the chance of identity theft.

The Executor Help Solution

The biggest dangers and problems that cause stress:

- Not having access to all the digital assets logins.
- Avoiding online theft.
- Not shutting down all social media accounts.

What you need to do and where to get the help:

- Create a list of all digital assets and keep it in a safe place.
- Find out what accounts exist and need to be deleted.

How this helps you:

- This is one more important job you will be able to complete fairly quickly.
- You won't have to worry about identity theft.

Chapter 9
How to have the conversation when you're the executor

Grace and Alex recently noticed their parents were slowing down.

Their father in his late seventies and was partially blind and the mother was losing her hearing. Recently, she fell and broke her hip.

They still lived in the family home. Grace and Alex lived in the same city as their parents but did not live close by.

They were concerned about their parents' living arrangements but had no idea how to bring up the subject or how to talk to their parents about getting their affairs in order.

Their father was defiant and would repeatedly say he would not live anywhere where there are rules, like at an assisted living residence.

He would just buy a different house if he had to accommodate his wife's recent injury.

Grace and Alex feel their father is acting this way because he feels he is losing his independence.

Due to the heaviness of the subject, Grace and Alex had no idea what to do.

No one ever wants to talk about their parents dying, but if something were to happen to their parents, they do not want to be scrambling, trying to figure out what they should do.

I know exactly how they feel. I never had the courage to have the conversation with my parents until it was too late.

We had noticed my dad was not himself, and it got to the point where one evening we had a family intervention about his behavior and the hurtful things he was saying to my mom.

He was argumentative and firm in his delusional beliefs.

I remember driving home sad.

When I walked into the house, I said to Susan, "I know my dad and that guy I was talking to was not him."

Then one Saturday night, my father threatened the life of my mother.

Thankfully, he did not act on his thoughts, but that was the last straw for my sister and me.

We would never be able to live with ourselves if we did not do something.

The next day was Father's Day, so I picked him up at church and told him we were going out for a celebratory lunch, when, in fact, I was taking him to the hospital.

He never got to go back home or live with my mother after more than thirty years of marriage.

He always blamed me for his predicament and believed there was nothing ever wrong with him until his dying day.

He would yell at me every time I went to see him, and it hurt, but I knew I did the right thing to protect him and my mother.

Since then, Father's Day has never meant the same to me because of what I had to do to keep my parents safe.

In his book, *When Roles Reverse*, author Jim Comer says there is no ideal time to tackle hard stuff.

Just as we don't schedule a stomach virus for next Tuesday, there will never be a perfect day to ask a parent to hand over the car keys.

At some point, we must put the taboo on the table.

For example, intensive care is not the place to discover that Dad doesn't have a will.

There are no meaningful discussions with someone on a respirator.

We need to communicate early and often.

To parent our parents successfully, we must first realize that they need our help. While denial is natural, there are times we need to take the initiative and risk causing raised voices and tears.

It's better to cause a scene than to ignore the truth. Never minimize the effects of aging and loss.

Understand how painful it is for one parent to watch the other lose health or memory.

I wish I had the courage earlier and wasn't afraid of confrontation. Even though they had a will, I should have gotten them to communicate to all family members to make it known that their wishes were an equal split.

That would have saved my sister and me seven years to settle the estate, ten court appearances, and $50,000 in lawyer fees.

Psychologist Marianne Van Oyen recommends Grace and Alex should first speak together about how they feel about what is happening with their parents.

What are they up for?

What are their boundaries?

What do their parents want?

Are they on the same page, or is their mother open to moving to a residence?

What is the parents' financial situation?

Can they afford services if they want to stay in their home?

Once this information has been assessed and established, Grace and Alex need to set up a meeting with their parents—perhaps over coffee, lunch, or dinner—and state that they would like to discuss how their parents are feeling about everything.

Grace and Alex can share their concerns with their parents so that they realize that if something should happen, their children cannot regularly drop everything to run to their aid.

If there are adequate funds to purchase help and support, then that could be a solution, as living in a residence can be very costly and the care is not always great.

At the same time, they can broach what their parents will want medically, in case something happens to them.

Do they have a living will?

Do they have a will?

The kids can preface this information by discussing their own wills and the importance of having one, just in case.

Otherwise, monies will be held up or forgotten in the shuffle, accounts will be frozen, and no clear guidelines around the parents' wishes will be available.

Ultimately it is the parents' decision to move or not or to have a will; however, it is also the responsibility of their children to set their limits, expectations, and boundaries.

A few therapy sessions could help the process, if they get stuck.

The greatest compliment we can pay our parents is to be honest with them and do the things we have to do to keep them safe.

The Executor Help Solution

The biggest dangers and problems that cause stress:

- You are reluctant to have a conversation with your parents when you see things changing.
- You procrastinate.
- You are being apathetic.

What you need to do and where to get the help:

- Get together with siblings and get on the same page.
- Discuss your feelings with your parents.
- If needed, seek professional help.

How this helps you:

- You would have done the right things to keep your parents safe.
- You will let them know how much you love them.
- You will sleep more soundly knowing you did your best.

Chapter 10
What to do with the furry members of the family?

Ethan was the executor of his mother's estate; he was a beneficiary, along with his sister Allison.

It was his mother's wish the estate be split evenly.

Allison had a hard time dealing with the loss of her mom, and she was continuously taking things out of the house because she needed to hold on to her mom.

Their mom, Claire, was the glue of the family; she organized all the family get-togethers.

Everyone knew they could count on her.

For a while, her nephew Kevin, his wife, and newborn lived with her.

She had two dogs. One was a foster and the other a rescue.

When Claire died, Kevin assumed he would take the dogs since he lived in the house, wanted the responsibility, and loved dogs.

Unfortunately, this became an emotional issue with his cousin Allison.

She believed the dogs were part of her family and they should both go with her.

This put Ethan in the middle of the dispute. He did not want to fight with his sister because he saw she was hurting.

But he knew he had to find a solution for the sake of the dogs.

So, he pointed out to his sister that if she really wanted to take both dogs, she needed to think long and hard. She needed to be honest with herself, understand the older dog had issues, and realize there was a huge financial commitment to having both.

After thinking about the reality and responsibility, Allison decided to take only the older dog as it was the one she and her mother picked together when she was a child.

People feel very strongly about their pets. This can become another headache for the executor if there is no guidance.

Lesley Nase is an intuitive animal healer, and she says that an executor should have a clear idea. You have to ask questions. If you're going to be the executor, make sure that besides knowing how to deal with the financial assets, you also know how to deal with the pets.

What often happens is they end up being surrendered to a shelter.

That's because there is no instruction in the will or any verbal agreement from anyone about is going to take the bird, dog, cat, or horses when the testator died.

It will be an emotional time for you as executor.

But when you have it all written out and agreed, everything is made easier.

When Margaret's cancer returned for a third time, she wanted to make sure the love of her life, Java, would be taken care of.

Through her cancer battle, she appreciated how her little dog did more for her than anyone.

Java made her feel safe and loved, and all Margaret wanted was to make sure Java would be safe when she was no longer there to cuddle her.

She had two executors of her estate. She had an idea of where she wanted the dog to go and told them exactly what the best situation was for her Java.

She knew she was leaving her and wanted to do what was the best for the pet.

As part of her estate planning, she was able to not only pick Java's next owner, but that person was already active in the dog's life.

She also left a portion of her money for the care of Java. It was a trust fund that covered food, burial, or anything else the dog should need.

This was important for Java's transition. She was going to a new home and it was with a couple she knew.

This would be the ideal situation—a person(s) in the animal's life willing to take them. But that's not always the case

The Executor Help Solution

The biggest dangers and problems that cause stress:

- You have no instructions on what to do with the pets.
- There is a fight for the pets.
- No one wants to take the pets.

What you need to do and where to get the help:

- Right after death, you need to take care of the animals until the will is read.
- If you have no instructions ask family, friends if they will take the pet(s).
- Check out the best shelter.

How this helps you:

- You know the animals are being taken care of.
- They can bring you some comfort.

Chapter 11
Cottages and other vacation properties

Cam's mom and dad retired to the family cottage on a bay in the Muskoka region when his dad was 57. It was at first a very small cottage, but it was being worked on to be their permanent home

All of the eight kids were welcome there. That's where everybody loved to go to see Mom and Dad.

When I talked to Cam over Zoom while researching this book, I heard his full story for the first time.

I always remembered what a good listener he was any time I would go off on my own problems with an unreasonable and entitled sibling.

He always seemed to understand what I was going through; I had no idea how much we had in common.

He went through a difficult time when his parents died.

I wanted to let him know that he was not the only one.

He said, "I'm not affected like I used to be, but it still bothers me that it's an open wound that never goes away. The carnage and wreckage is there for good."

Of course, there are elements of the estate triangle of conflict in this story; in this case, siblings who feel entitled to unearned wealth and forget to see each other as human beings.

The other crucial element you'll discover in the chapter on the importance of estate planning.

Up at the cottage, Cam loved helping his dad open things up for the summer, fix and launch the boats, hang out, and play cribbage, where Dad always kicked his butt.

He did not mind being the only one who ever went up to the cottage and actually did any work. He just did what he had to do because he loved his mom and dad.

That's what you are supposed to do.

The family cottage or any other vacation property can be a source of hard feelings, stress, and conflict.

As the executor, you need to be aware of what the will says on how it will be handled. Is it going to stay in the family?

When his mom and dad died, two of his brothers took on the role of executors and then proceeded to do everything you are not supposed to do when you have taken on the responsibility.

They produced a letter with some questionable signatures of administration before their mother died.

Right at the start, the brothers let everyone know they were going to be claiming executor fees. They would never disclose the amount. "Well, you don't need to know that amount," they said.

Within a month, Cam knew that something had to happen because now they were all faced with having to pay bills and the executors did nothing.

It got to the point where they didn't even make the taxes and the insurance on the property.

And they didn't manage any of the investments.

Plus, the executors were not communicating with the beneficiaries.

The siblings began to take sides.

Cam wanted to have a conversation with his brothers about how the estate was being managed and their executor fees.

Their next move was to immediately get a lawyer.

While lawyers became part of the estate battle, Cam and his wife continued to manage the cottage.

He continued the construction work he loved doing alongside his dad. I am pretty sure it gave him comfort.

As the bills mounted and were not being paid by the brothers, Cam was forced to get his own lawyer.

He wanted to force his brothers to produce a complete accounting of what was happening in the estate.

Cam's lawyer advised against going to court as the lawyer fees on both sides would eat up the value of the estate and leave about $50,000, which would, at the end, have to be split among the eight siblings.

Everyone in the family knew that Cam's dad always wanted the cottage to stay in the family.

Yet while everybody was grieving, the brothers did the unthinkable and sold the cottage.

"With Mum and Dad gone, they can't say anything to us. It's our time to grab a slice," is how Cam viewed his brothers' actions.

I can relate to when a sibling does something that they know their parents would not ever agree to.

But then again, equal is not always fair in their mind.

His brothers being faced with court action on how they mismanaged the estate and the threat of being sued for negligence by Cam.

The entitled brothers knew they were not going to win in court. Their lawyers told them as much.

It took four years to settle the estate and over $45,000 in lawyer fees for Cam.

Not to mention what it cost his brothers.

In his book, *Bobby Gets Bubkes*, lawyer Charles B. Ticker says there is only one reason cases get settled.

People run out of steam and money. Estate litigation is extremely expensive.

He adds that it takes a tremendous emotional toll on the parties.

In estate litigation cases, the parties are constantly reliving bad memories, such as fights with siblings and the loss of their parents.

- As executor, you need to pay special attention to how a second property like a cottage is mentioned in the will.
- Ask the testator (person making the will) what their wishes are.

- Ask your accountant what tax issues will emerge.
- What is going to happen to the property if it is sold or transferred to someone else?
- What happens if one of the future owners can't afford to pay for their share of expenses? Or if they get divorced, become mentally incompetent, or die?

Today Cam speaks to one sister and socializes with her. Some of the other siblings stay in contact with the brothers.

One has tried to reach out to him on Facebook, but Cam cannot find it in himself to be his friend. He thinks even less of his younger brother.

"They just didn't give a shit about Mom and Dad's thoughts, their goals, and their wishes. They only cared about themselves, not their parents. This would have broken their hearts. It would hurt my dad. It would hurt my mom."

Cam advocates being really clear about what happens to the family cottage, and staying away from court. "This is a money maker for lawyers. This is what buys their cottages."

The Executor Help Solution

The biggest dangers and problems that cause stress:

- You don't know what the wishes of the testator are for the cottage.
- You don't know what the tax situation will be.
- How to manage the property until a decision is made.
- What you need to do and where to get the help.
- Talk to your accountant and have them explain the tax implications.
- Communicate only with the beneficiaries (no spouses, cousins, or other family members) of the cottage.
- If a dispute comes up, get a mediator before heading to court

How this helps you:

- You will have an understanding of how this could affect the tax return you have to file.
- You will have let beneficiaries know how this will affect them.
- You'll avoid going to court and paying hefty lawyer fees.

Chapter 12
What to do if there is a business

Ian retired from machine sales and lived on his houseboat on the Lachine Canal in Quebec, Canada.

He would often tell me how people confessed to him how they would do ANYTHING to have his lifestyle.

There's simply nothing better than spending a great day out on the water, watching the sunset on the horizon, and realizing that it was another beautiful day filled with some UNFORGETTABLE memories.

When the cold wind started to blow, he and his little dog, Zoey, would get in his RV and spend the winters in Florida.

To me, what made Ian's lifestyle so unique was he was able to turn his love of houseboats into a business.

Houseboating for him started when he was a young kid. His dad suggested they should build a houseboat.

He was thrilled with the idea and still remembered those special times they spent building the boat together.

He decided to create a houseboat website, www.all-about-house-boats.com, but little did he know that it would become one of the most popular houseboat websites on the internet.

The website receives thousands of daily visitors, and provides active readers with a huge variety of houseboat related topics.

In the summer of 2017, I sat on the deck of the houseboat with Ian, had a couple of beers, and laughed.

We also talked about his stage 4 cancer diagnoses.

He never lost his sense of humor. He was only concerned about his wife, Linda, and his dog, Zoey.

I asked him what was going to happen to the online business.

He told me he wanted Linda to run it and was taking steps to show her how the business operated.

The problem was, Linda loved living on a houseboat, but had no idea about running an online houseboat business.

When you are an executor for someone who also ran a business, you will have to assume a lot of other responsibilities. These other responsibilities are likely to cause you additional stress.

When Ian passed away in March 2018, Linda was his executor. He made sure Zoey was going to be taken care of by a close friend, who also inherited the houseboat.

Fortunately, Linda was able to find the name of someone in Ian's wallet who could run the online business with her.

A lot of executors in this situation, they are not so lucky. When the testator (the one who wrote the will) dies, so does the business.

But as executor, you are going to be the one who has to shut the business down and get in touch with customers and suppliers.

Imagine how much more complicated the job would be if this were a corporation?

In this case, you are going to have to rely heavily on the lawyer and the accountant who are familiar with the structure of the company.

Every business is different and, while entrepreneurs love doing things themselves, you will have to make decisions in many cases by guessing what was in the mind of the now-deceased owner.

- Is there someone who knows the business and can run it?
- Can you sell the business?
- Do you shut down the business?

Hopefully, the owner took the time to also have a succession plan.

More on why it is so important for business owners, whether they are incorporated or not, to have a succession plan can be found in the planning your estate section.

The Executor Help Solution

The biggest dangers and problems that cause stress:

- You don't know where to start.
- You are getting contacted by clients and suppliers.
- You can't find the succession plan.

What you need to do and where to get the help:

- Contact lawyer for the company (succession plan).
- Contact accountant of the company (taxes).
- Follow the will.

How this helps you:

- You have professionals working for you who you can rely on.

Chapter 13
How to have a conversation with your executor

Katherine and Robert are retirees, married for decades, and fairly well along in years, but in good health.

They have a decent estate of cash, securities, house, and lots of "stuff"—more wealth than most people their age.

They recently updated their wills to indicate whichever one of them survives, the other gets everything.

Much of their wealth is designated to go to their four kids equally and some specific charities after they are both gone.

They have never talked about this with their adult children.

They need help in bringing up the conversation. To them, it is scary.

I find that as people take a closer look at their estates and their wishes, it is not uncommon for them to struggle with this conversation.

Author Cindy Arledge in her book, *The Legacy Family Way*, says for the vast majority of people, death is a topic to avoid.

Not surprisingly, avoidance is at the heart of the problem.

She says sadly, society has accepted failed inheritances as normal. By breaking the taboo on discussing death and money, you will gain an understanding of the real issue and access to a viable solution

How should Katherine and Robert approach their children about their estate plans and not make them feel uncomfortable?

What should they say and how do they say it so their children know what their wishes are?

Psychologist Marianne Van Oyen says the parents can casually have a conversation with their children by discussing this topic over dinner or when the occasion presents itself.

Parents might simply state, in passing, they had their wills updated and mention who they have named as the executor.

Depending on the reaction of the children, for example, they will know if their children are interested to know more or if they have specific questions.

She said it would be a good opportunity to give more details about the will and perhaps decide on a mutually convenient time to sit down and go over the will in more detail and discuss where important information can be located regarding assets, debts, investments, valuable, insurance policies, etc.

Although uncomfortable, it can be a relief for adult children to know that their parents have a will and where they can access all the pertinent information before a crisis were to strike.

Especially today, with COVID-19 breathing down people's necks, one never knows what can happen, she added.

If the children are not available for any kind of conversation about this topic in the moment, then the parents can suggest finding a mutually convenient time to discuss the details.

Emphasize how important it is to review in the event that anything ever happens.

Let the children know where this material is kept and provide all the contact information for the children to have access to in case something happens.

The parents must also make their wishes clear that all of the children are considered in their wills, and they anticipate no arguing over the money and valuables.

If there a reason for it not being equal due to a loan to a child or a family business, this is the time to discuss your reasoning.

It may also be a good idea to have the children let their parents know what they might like to inherit so that it is clear to everyone in the family unit to avoid arguments in the future.

Having this conversation is part of what Arledge calls Family Legacy Planning. "Don't fail to communicate because everyone appears to 'get along.'" Don't fool yourself.

She adds that you cannot anticipate how your family will respond to their inheritance until after it happens. And then, it's too late.

When siblings can let go of childhood hurts, remove rose-colored glasses, or pain goggles, and find common ground between different lifestyles, they are better prepared to communicate and trust each other after you are gone.

Ideally, your family members like each other, but at a minimum, accepting each other and agreeing to respect each other now, WHILE YOU ARE ALIVE, will prepare them for the future when your stabilizing presence is gone.

The Executor Help Solution

The biggest dangers and problems that cause stress:

- Not having a conversation with your heirs.
- You don't let your wishes be known.
- You believe everyone "gets along," so there is no need to talk.

What you need to do and where to get the help:
- Get your family together.
- Let your wishes be known.
- Let them know where this information is kept.

How this helps you:

- You know the people who love and care for you understand what you want.

Chapter 14
If you have a business, you need a succession plan

Susan and I love going to Vegas at least once year, but not to gamble since neither one of us are good at the tables. (Roulette is actually our favorite.)

We just love two- or three-days maximum excitement of the place, the restaurants (I am a foodie), shows, and driving out in the desert. Our favorite thing to do is sit at an outdoor table at a restaurant, Mon Ami Gabi at the Paris Hotel.

This way, we can enjoy the steak frites, watch the fountain show across the street at the Bellagio, and people watch.

Over the years, we really have seen a huge change for the better in the downtown area that is not the strip.

This part of Las Vegas used to be a bit sketchy to walk around at night.

It was where Tony Hsieh, CEO of Zappos, an online shoe retailer, moved his headquarters.

He worked hard to re-vitalize the area to lure companies to the desert.

Like many entrepreneurs who are so successful and focused on the business, they don't always take the time to focus on themselves and be prepared for the unplanned.

There is no motivation to think about estate planning and, more importantly, a succession plan. Which means they are either reluctant, procrastinating or just plain apathetic.

Every business in the world has at least one thing in common: it needs someone in charge in order to succeed.

On July 22, 2009, Amazon acquired Zappos.com in a deal valued at approximately $1.2 billion. Hsieh is said to have made at least $214 million from the sale.

On August 24, 2020, Hsieh, at age 46, retired as the CEO of Zappos after twenty-one years.

On the morning of November 18, 2020, Tony Hsieh was injured in a house fire. He died on November 27, two weeks before his 47th birthday.

Estimated net worth $850 million.

No will.

No succession plan.

For all the good Tony Hsieh did and the outpouring of support from around the world following the news of his passing, he left a mess for his family, who are still getting over his surprising death.

It was reported there was no will, but none of his family or associates are really sure.

Even when a person has a will, it doesn't have much value if others aren't aware of it and where it can be located.

As for executors, a cousin petitioned a court to be named guardian of Hsieh and his estate after he was injured in the fire.

Then, after his death, a Las Vegas judge appointed Hsieh's father and brother to act as special administrators and representatives of the estate.

Here is another ingredient from the estate triangle of conflict.

No Will.

What could possibly go wrong?

Business Owners: Don't Leave Your Executors in the Dark.

It has been reported that when the executors entered his home, they found business deals scrawled on thousands of Post-it notes covering his walls.

Without a will to follow, the executors now must try to trace Hsieh's full worth and recent business dealings—with his most recent investments made through a dozen limited-liability companies.

There are apparently numerous projects in various stages of development, and there's some question about the extent of charitable commitments Hsieh made in both Las Vegas, Nevada, and Park City, Utah.

You don't think there are going to be lawsuits?

Hsieh didn't leave a master list or inventory of his assets and liabilities.

With or without a business, everyone should create and update such a list.

The inventory makes it easier to develop your estate plan and, more importantly, gives the executor some sort of a guide to settling the estate.

Since Hsieh didn't leave an inventory of his estate, his administrators will spend months and perhaps years simply identifying the assets and liabilities.

In addition, some of the assets are likely to lose value in the time it takes for the estate to determine they are part of the estate and begin managing them.

Let's approach death and possible incapacity from a personal perspective.

Say you own a business or a percentage of a business.

You may have a successful company you fund and operate on your own, or a team of people you've partnered with.

Either way, it's up to you to make sure all your bases are covered, which includes estate and succession planning.

What do you want to happen to your business?

Some business owners I've asked this question of have the mindset the business will die when they do.

Then there are the owners who value all the time, sweat, and tears they've poured into their work and hope it will sustain their family even after they are gone.

I know this is not the most glamorous of decisions you have to make, but some would argue it's one of the most important.

- Is there someone who knows the business and can run it?
- Do you want the business sold?
- Do you want the business to shut down?

The answers you have in your head do not make it a succession plan nor does it help those you leave behind.

If your business' income supports your family and they couldn't survive without it, consider getting life insurance to supplement some of that income when you're gone.

This is even a good idea if you do have a successor to take over the business.

You can never be too secure when it comes to your business and family's future.

Do you have a way to protect your family?

Are you comfortable leaving them unprepared, lost, unorganized?

The Executor Help Solution

The biggest dangers and problems that cause stress:

- No plan for the business if you become incapacitated or die.
- Who is in charge if you are not there?
- What does your family do?

What you need to do and where to get the help:

- Create an estate plan.
- Create a succession plan and update it regularly with your lawyer and accountant as circumstances change in the business.
- Work with your lawyer and an insurance professional.

How this helps you:

- You'll feel confident knowing you have planned in case of an emergency.
- The business can function.
- Your family will not be lost or disorganized.

Chapter 15
10 reasons to have an estate plan

Cam's dad didn't see death coming. He didn't know that a truck was going to take him out while he was just out getting something for his wife.

He had no idea he was not going to return home. It was almost six months to the day since his mother had a major stroke while she was in California.

His parents didn't have any out of country insurance. So, they had to stabilize her to get her back to Canada.

That event essentially bankrupted them.

By the time all eight children came together, his mom had not seen her husband for five days. She was looking around the room for him and when they told her, she was crushed.

Because of her condition, she was never able to tell them if there was a will somewhere.

Cam's mom lived for another five years after her massive stroke. During that time, everyone searched the family home to find a copy of a will.

No one found anything, and this created a unique problem.

Cam admitted his dad and mom should have written a will. Let everyone what their wishes were.

Cam said, "There would not have been the breakdown in the family like there is today, if my parents had said, on our death, sell

93

the cottage, or if they had something else lined up. But they had nothing." He went on to say:

> If you've got any kind of wealth, even a car, and you die, make sure somebody knows who is going to get the car.
> If you've got any assets, do the right thing and just get a lawyer involved to handle it all so there's no questions.
> Have the conversation (with family), it's uncomfortable but get the conversation over and done with.
> Put it out in the open, make a file visible so somebody could trip over it.
> Make sure people know they're going to see this folder.
> The file has to contain the information an executor is going to need, because you don't want people hunting down things.
> When people die, it's traumatic and you're not going to find a folder in the middle of trauma, if it's hidden somewhere. It's got to be easy to find by the right people.
> If you want your kids to have friendships and family after your passing, do the right thing.
> [If you forgot how Cam's family ended up broken, re-read the cottages and vacation properties chapter.]
> Make a will and make sure you have a power of attorney for your health as well.
> Do those things and you will help your family more than you helped them with their diaper changes.

Having an up-to-date estate plan with a valid will helps to ensure that your dependents and heirs will be provided for according to your wishes.

Reasons to have an estate plan

- Provide adequately for your spouse and dependents.
- Distribute assets according to your wishes, not the courts.
- With an estate plan, you choose the guardian for your minor children and their care, not the courts.

Danielle understood the importance of having a will and estate planning.

Her situation is simple. With no children, she has named her longtime friend Rachel as executor, and Rachel knows where the will is kept. Her assets are to be split with Rachel and her brother. She also has power of attorney in case of incapacity.

Also, to make sure that her business will continue until a buyer is found, there is a succession plan.

As a successful business owner, Danielle wanted to make sure she did not repeat her parents' mistakes when, as a child, her future was decided in the parking lot of a funeral home.

When Danielle's father died at age 39, she was only 12.

This is where things get complicated.

> When my dad passed away with no will, my grand-
> father's estate was not yet settled and my great-
> grandfather's estate was not yet settled.
> So, we're talking three generations of estates not
> settled, but the one thing they all had in common is
> that there was no will.

Danielle's family was large, so it was decided in the parking lot of the funeral home that one aunt and uncle would take her.

Another aunt and uncle took her brother.

Danielle has memories of a happy childhood. She felt she never missed out on anything.

She credits her aunt and uncle for making her the strong, confident woman she is today.

Though it was extremely time-consuming and at times painful for them. Since there was no will, the government was in control of the money.

Every time they needed money for her care, they had to go to court and explain what every dollar was being used for.

If you are concerned with what will happens to your pets, Authors Barry Seltzer and Gerry W. Beyer, in their book, *Fat Cats and Lucky Dogs*, say there are at least five key occasions when your pet is danger:

1. When you are incapacitated and are unable to care for your pet.
2. Immediately after you die and your pets are at home alone, perhaps for days.
3. During the time between your death and when your will is read.
4. During the time between your will is read and when it is probated.
5. The ongoing period after your will is probated.

An estate plan means you choose the guardian for your pets and their care.

You get to write a power of attorney and choose who will manage your affairs.

You can reduce or defer taxes.

You can reduce probate, legal, and executor fees.

You can provide funds for all final expenses and liabilities

When Claire's husband died of cancer, he didn't tell her in hindsight what he had done for her.

She remembers him working on the cottage, even when it was difficult to do so. He did all the renovations that needed to be done.

At the time, it didn't really click what he was doing. After he died, she found a folder on his dresser with everything that she needed to know about his holdings, such as investments, insurance policies, etc.

Everything was in that folder, all nicely all laid out. She didn't have to scramble around.

It lessened what she had to go through coping with the loss and the stress. He made his being gone a lot easier on her. He never told her he was going, but once he was gone, everything was organized.

An estate plan decreases the time and potential problems to settle your estate.

You decide how to pass on your business to your spouse, children, partner, or other party.

You get to gift money or assets to the charities of your choice

Estate planning is not just for rich people; it's an opportunity for people of any age to control who will inherit their money and property, and to decide who can make medical and financial decisions on their behalf if they're unable to do so themselves.

You need to make a lot of estate-planning decisions. Even young people (single ones too), just starting out, should have some key documents to make their wishes known if anything happens to them.

Since the coronavirus pandemic has become a threat to us all, it has made more people realize the importance of being prepared for the unexpected at any age.

The Executor Help Solution

The biggest dangers and problems that cause stress:

- You have not taken the time to prepare for the unexpected.
- You do not have a will.
- You have not done all you can to protect your family.

What you need to do and where to get the help:

- Meet with a lawyer or notary.
- Prepare an estate plan, which includes a will.
- Make health care directives.
- Make a financial power of attorney.
- Let your family know when these important documents are kept.

How this helps you:

- You can rest easy knowing you have prepared your family in case an unexpected emergency occurs.
- You have had the conversations that need to be had.
- The family knows where this important information is kept.

10 Things to prepare to be asked
when planning your estate

Most initial meetings when planning an estate will result in some questions you have likely never considered.

To help you get prepared and save time, here are some questions to consider and information to gather in advance.

1. Who will be your executor(s)?
2. If you have minor children, who would you want as guardians?
3. Who are your beneficiaries, and how do you want your estate distributed among them?
4. Who will be your patient advocate to make medical decisions for you if you are unable to do so?
5. Are there any charitable bequests you would like to make?
6. Are there any special personal property items (e.g., cars, clothing, jewelry, artwork, collectibles, etc.) that you would like to be given to a specific person?
7. If you have pets, who should be named to care for them, and will you leave any funds in trust for their ongoing care?
8. If you have a business, what would you like to happen to it? Keep it in the family? Have a key employee run it? Sell it? Close it down?
9. If one of your beneficiaries dies before you, what should happen to their share?
10. Have you got information regarding your assets? It is rarely necessary to have complete statement balances for all of your assets, but knowing what types of assets you have and your total net worth is very important to properly plan your estate.

Chapter 16
How to pick an executor

William's cousin Daniel found his dad a place to live, as he needed more monitoring as he was slowing down.

He was also forgetting things, so it made sense they set up a joint bank account so bills would be paid. This is not uncommon when one child is also the executor.

Daniel took over the job when William refused to be executor. (Remember why William declined in the chapter, The truth about being chosen as an executor, welcome to "the shit show.")

However, whether it's intentional or not, the majority of banks, when you set up a joint account, is with right of survivorship.

Be sure to ask for no right of survivorship.

With right of survivorship, all you need to do is produce a death certificate and the money in the bank accounts automatically goes to the survivor of that account.

Parents just want to make it easier for their kids to pay bills. But what ends up happening, unfortunately, is the child who has access to the joint account usually takes the money.

The other siblings can't fight it as the parent signed the joint account agreements, making it all legal.

Due to his failing health, his dad moved to a retirement home and paid bills through his joint checking account.

This is where all of his pension income would be deposited.

At the time of his death, there was well over $100,000 in the account.

The estate consisted of a small retirement investment account and some stocks.

Daniel never produced an asset and liability statement.

There was always tension among the siblings, so when it came time to distribute to beneficiaries, the money in the bank account was not counted as part of the assets.

The beneficiaries wanted to go to court to fight to add the money in the bank account.

While it was probably not what their father would want, the bank did nothing wrong. The beneficiaries had no case.

Maybe you think a member of your immediate family—perhaps your spouse or oldest child—would serve as the executor of your estate.

Or you may choose a close friend to handle these duties.

After reading this book, you might realize that the person you assume would be the obvious choice might not be the best one for the job

Now, what do you do?

1. For you to pick "right" person(s) for the role of executor. First, be sure that your top choice is willing to do the job and they understand what is being asked of them.
   It should be someone who is younger than you and lives nearby.
2. You have prepared a file for your executor; you've made it easy for them to find. You should keep at least two copies of the file, a printed version in a safe and the other on a secure digital document on a hard drive or backup drive in a safe location.
   In the file include: your will, usernames and passwords, key contacts (such as lawyer, accountant, financial adviser, for example), bank account information, and insurance details.
3. If you would rather not go the do it yourself (DIY) route, I would strongly suggest a corporate executor, especially if your estate will be complicated—an incorporated business, lots of properties and investments, and elements of the triangle of conflict. A corporate executor has the knowledge to handle

complex trust, estate, and tax issues. They will have their own team. They will be impartial and won't be part of the family drama, which is good and bad, as some family members might be ignored. Corporate executors don't come cheap. They will charge a fee for their work, which may be a concern as the fees will reduce the value of the estate to be distributed to beneficiaries. It is general practice to charge fees based on the value of the estate as well as earnings in the estate. People who go this route have a corporate executor as the co-executor with a family or friend. This way, the threat of family drama can be addressed and minimized.

So, what's the right answer? DIY or corporate executor?

David Chilton, author of probably one of the greatest books on personal finance ever written in Canada and the US, *The Wealthy Barber* (knowing Dave, he would sheepishly and humbly agree), is not a fan of the DIY. He is a big fan of the corporate executor. He does not want his kids to be his executor as he says it is too much work, too much stress, too much financial liability, and can lead to family breakdown.

By now, you know what it takes to be an executor, and you know why it is so important to do proper estate planning.

There is no one right answer as every estate is different, but elements for it be a nightmare are always present (the estate triangle of conflict).

And even if you have an estate plan, it needs to be reviewed and updated every two years or whenever your circumstances change.

Keep it current.

Keep it up to date

You need to do what is the best for your family so you do not leave them unprepared, lost, and unorganized.

The Executor Help Solution

The biggest dangers and problems that cause stress:

- You have not taken your estate planning seriously.
- You have not picked your executor(s).
- You have not prepared your executor for the job.

What you need to do and where to get the help:

- Create or review your estate plan.
- Prepare a file for your executor and make it easy to find.
- Make at least two copies of the file: a printed version and a secure digital document on a hard drive or backup drive in a safe location.
- If you would rather not just have one executor, consider a corporate executor. Still, prepare a file for them.

How this helps you:

- You've done your best to prepare your family during a time of trauma.
- You've prepared your executor.
- You have taken care of this unpleasant task, finally.

Chapter 17
The 50 most common executor questions answered

1. Do executors get paid?

The various provincial and territorial Trustee Acts across Canada stipulate that a trustee is entitled to such fair and reasonable financial allowance. There is no fixed rate of compensation applicable under all circumstances for the services of trustees. The Canada Revenue Agency regards compensation received by an executor to be taxable income.

In the United States, it varies from state to state and can be calculated as a percentage of the estate, a flat fee, or an hourly rate, according to state law.

2. Do an estate's co-executors have to agree unanimously on how to proceed?

Yes. Where there are several trustees acting as co-executors, they must unanimously agree on the steps to settle the estate. No law enables the majority of trustees to bind the minority.

The co-executors must decide unanimously on each step, unless the will specifies another acceptable form of decision-making process to work out possible differences of opinion among the co-executors.

3. Do I have to accept to be an executor of a will? (If not, what do I have to do to decline?)

In Canada, as long as you have not applied for probate or started to administer the estate, you can decline your role as executor by filing with the estates court. It is a fairly straightforward process that involves signing a form.

The same for the United States. Declining the nomination is usually quite simple, if you act immediately. You can renounce the position by signing and filing a simple form with the probate court before you start to act for the estate. Many states offer renunciation forms online.

4. How can a beneficiary challenge the executor of a will? (Does this differ in each state, province/territory?)

An executor has a fiduciary duty to the estate and its beneficiaries. As such, the executor's actions may be challenged in court on the basis that they breached this duty. The court also has the inherent jurisdiction to remove and replace executors, but it will not interfere with the expressed wishes of the deceased without significant reason.

5. Is it mandatory for the executor to give each beneficiary a copy of the will? (If not, how does a beneficiary obtain a copy?)

No, it is not mandatory for the executor to provide the beneficiaries with a copy of the will. However, the will becomes public record once probate (the process whereby the will is proved in court to be legitimate) is granted.

For a number of pragmatic reasons, an executor may wish to share the contents of the will with a beneficiary.

6. Isn't it always best for the executor to hire a lawyer to help with the estate settlement?

It is not always necessary for an executor to hire a lawyer. A typical estate with common assets, such as a home, bank accounts, and insurance policies, requires mostly the completion of standard paperwork, which an executor can easily handle.

However, when an estate's assets are atypical, such as a business, then the executor may need to hire a lawyer. Or, if the person who wrote the will was involved in either financial disputes or more complicated property/business partnerships that require a decision by a judge, a lawyer might also be required.

7. Is an executor required to keep beneficiaries informed about the progress being made in the estate's settlement, or can they simply be contacted once everything is done?

The executor of a will is a trustee and fiduciary, which means that the executor does not own the estate, nor any of its assets. The executor is simply a custodian and manager of the still unsettled estate.

Since the estate's assets will ultimately belong to the beneficiaries, the executor has a responsibility to keep them informed within reasonable time frames and to account for any actions taken on behalf of the estate and/or the beneficiaries.

An executor can send periodic emails (perhaps weekly or every second week) to the beneficiaries, informing them about any new developments, updating them on the progress toward the estate's settlement, and disclosing all the financial accounting information in full in relation to the estate's assets.

8. Shouldn't a lawyer ideally be appointed as the executor?

You can appoint a lawyer as an executor, but consider the advantages and disadvantages of doing so.

First of all, understand that this is the appointment of an executor, who happens to be a lawyer, in the same way that a doctor or a mechanic might be appointed to be the executor. The lawyer's responsibilities would only extend to those of an executor, even though the lawyer might have additional legal and/or estate management knowledge/experience.

A lawyer is likely to be more impartial and objective in the execution of estate duties in ways that a relative or a close family friend may not be able to manage. A lawyer may also have specialized skills, such as attention to detail, which may be beneficial.

However, if this lawyer is not a family relative or close friend of the person whose will it is, the lawyer is more likely to decline to be the executor or require greater compensation for their time.

Furthermore, it is essential for anyone selecting a lawyer (or other individual unrelated to the family) as the executor to realize that if that person dies before the will is executed, the executor named in that person's will may become the executor of this will, too. Therefore, it might be wiser to appoint a relative or close friend who has the deceased's and the beneficiaries' interests more at heart.

9. Should I take an executor's fee?

Yes, absolutely! The administration of an estate will require time and commitment, which entitle you to compensation.

The various Trustee Acts across the country provide that a trustee is entitled to such fair and reasonable allowance for care, pains, and trouble, and for time expended in and about the trust estate as may be allowed by the court.

There is no fixed rate of compensation applicable under all circumstances for the services of trustees.

Don't forget: the Canada Revenue Agency regards compensation received by an executor to be taxable income.

In the United States, it varies from state to state and can be calculated as a percentage of the estate, a flat fee, or an hourly rate according to state law. It will also be seen as taxable income.

10. What can an executor claim as expenses?

Executors can obtain reimbursement for any out-of-pocket costs incurred in relation to the estate's settlement, such as necessary travel, accommodations, payments toward the repair and maintenance of estate assets during the process of the estate's processing, as well as estate settlement costs, as long as these are reasonable and justifiable.

Receipts and other proofs of payments may not always be required, but it is extremely wise for an executor to maintain all records of incurred expenses in the event of a dispute.

11. What can an executor do and not do?

As the fiduciary, the executor must always prioritize the best interests of the estate. If precise details are not specified in the will, the executor may use reasonable initiative to make decisions as appropriate to the deceased's likely intentions.

An executor can:

Administer and distribute the estate in respect of which the personal representative is appointed,
a. Account to beneficiaries, creditors, and others to whom the personal representative has at law a duty to account, and
b. Perform any other duties imposed on the personal representative by the will of the deceased person or by law.

An executor cannot:

Change any of the terms of a will.

c. Personally, benefit from the estate unless the will names the executor as a beneficiary, and then only as specified by the will.
d. Stop beneficiaries from contesting the will.

12. What steps do I take as an executor once I accept this role?

Submit the will to the probate court for review and acceptance in order to officially begin the process.

a. Identify and gather documentation for all of the estate's assets.
b. Maintain the gathered documentation regarding all of the estate's assets.
c. Locate and inform the beneficiaries that they have been named in the will.
d. Decide if the services of the lawyer, accountant, financial adviser, real estate agent, and/or another professional are required.

13. What should an executor do first?

There are a number of approaches that are possible, depending on whether the person whose will it is remains alive or has already passed away.

If the person whose will it is remains alive, the executor's job can be made easier. With the permission of the individual whose will it is, the executor can arrange group meetings between the estate's owner and intended beneficiaries. This meeting is an opportunity for the estate's owner to share the details of the will and for the beneficiaries to air grievances, if any, regarding the planned distribution of wealth. This can give the estate's owner the opportunity to justify the planned distribution, if they want to do so. It also provides the opportunity for the estate's owner to subsequently make changes if someone or something was overlooked or has made a good case for the will's revision.

If the estate's owner is no longer living, the executor first has to determine whether the will needs to be filed for probate.

Some provinces do not require probate for estates whose assets, according to the will, are to be automatically transferred, such as a jointly owned home or bank accounts to a spouse.

Probate procedures typically depend on the size of the estate. In some provinces, minor estates with relatively few assets will have specific probate procedures compared to assets with more assets.

In the United States, go to probate court to file the will. The legal will of the deceased individual needs to be filed in a local probate court.

In some states, this isn't required in order for assets to be distributed, but most states will ask for this step to be completed.

14. What should an executor do when someone named in a will dies?

If a beneficiary dies before the estate is settled, the first step is to look at the will. Some wills will have a survival clause. It typically states that beneficiaries only become entitled to their gift if they survive the person's will by a specified amount of time.

However, if the will does not have a survival clause, some provinces have laws that set out a five-day survival rule. It states that if an intended beneficiary dies within five days of the death of the person whose will it is, that individual is deemed to have died before the person whose will is being settled.

If this is the case, some Succession Acts will determine whether a sibling, named alternative, or any surviving residuary beneficiaries are entitled to receive this gift.

If survival rules do not come into play, the deceased beneficiary's share reverts to the deceased's estate and is distributed according to the original will as it applies to the other beneficiaries or under the rules of intestacy (the conditions that apply to an estate that is left by a person who dies without having in force a valid will or other blinding declaration).

15. When can an executor or co-executor be removed?

Generally, there are only a few ways an executor or co-executor can be removed:

Voluntarily: If a person appointed as an executor or co-executor renounces probate of the will, that person's rights of executorship cease as if the person had not been appointed.

a. Failure to show: If an executor or co-executor survives the person whose will it is, but dies before that will is probated, the right of that person as executor or co-executor ceases as though the person had never been appointed to that role. The same goes for a named executor or co-executor who does not appear for a will's probate.

b. Right to apply for discharge: A personal representative of a deceased person may at any time apply to the court to be discharged from their office, as an executor or co-executor, and/or as an executor/co-executor and trustee. This application can be made whether the individual has been appointed as an executor/co-executor under the will or by the courts, either before or after a grant of the letters probate. A personal representative may make an application whether they have been appointed the executor under a will or by the courts, either before or after:

- A grant of letters probate (which officially confirms and registers that the named person is entitled to deal with the estate).
- A grant of letters of administration (the authority to administer the estate of an individual who has died without preparing a will).

c. Involuntary removal: In cases of proven/provable misconduct, courts of equity (i.e., courts authorized to apply principles of equity to the cases presented to it rather than the principles of law) have no difficulty in intervening to remove trustees who have abused their trust.

- Such action is only taken in cases of serious dereliction of duty. It is not done for every mistake or neglect of duty, or inaccuracy of conduct by a trustee.
- The acts or omissions must be such as to endanger the trust property or to show a want of honesty, or a want of proper capacity to execute the duties, or a want of reasonable fidelity.
- The interests of the beneficiaries are the court's primary concern. Any executor deemed to be acting in a manner that benefits them personally or to be detrimental to the beneficiaries could be viewed by the court as being in a conflict of interest and be removed.

16. Can someone who is a beneficiary of an estate also be the executor?

Yes. For example, a married or common-law couple without children can name each other as the beneficiary and executor of each other's estate in their wills.

However, this may become more complex if the beneficiary who is also named the executor has other financial or legal ties to the estate. For example, if the person acting as an executor is also a creditor of the estate. In such case, the executor will have to ensure that there is no conflict of interest in their execution of that role and also being a beneficiary.

If a conflict of interest is foreseeable before a will is written, it is advisable for the person making the will to appoint an independent third party as the executor. For instance, if a father is concerned that one of his three children will not otherwise be fairly compensated for working in the family business, then an independent third party might be a better choice as the will's executor.

If conflicts of interest arise after the person who made the will has died, it is advisable for the executor to seek legal advice.

17. When can an executor sell a property?

If a beneficiary has been located and notified by an executor of a specific gift but neglects or refuses to make arrangements to take delivery of the gifted property within a provincial/territorial statute's specified time (usually 180 days) of the notification, the executor may sell the property, deduct any costs related to the storage, transportation and/or sale of the property, and send the net proceeds in monetary funds to the beneficiary.

An executor can sell the property if a beneficiary cannot be located (usually within 12 months) of the date that probate has been granted for the will.

If a beneficiary does not wish to have a property for whatever reasons, the beneficiary may request the executor sell the property.

If beneficiaries to an estate have a dispute over a property and the court decides to affect a partition of property under the Partition of Property Acts, the executor may be mandated to sell the property with the proceeds (minus any involved storage, transportation, or sale costs) then distributed as instructed by a court.

An executor may sell a property immediately if named as the sole beneficiary of that property (once probate of the will is granted).

When a situation arises that requires an executor to sell a property, it is good practice for the executor to ensure that the property is evaluated by at least two independent, competent evaluators to determine the actual/best possible price for its sale.

The same advice applies if it is agreed that a beneficiary will obtain a property but equally compensate the other beneficiaries for their share of its value.

18. When can an executor sell investments?

An executor can sell an investment upon request by the named beneficiary of that particular investment or by court order.

An executor can also sell an investment if the appropriate time has elapsed since a beneficiary's or the beneficiaries' notification and they not making an effort to take delivery of the investment.

Additionally, if a beneficiary is not located (usually within 12 months), an executor may sell the investment, deduct costs related to the storage, transportation, and sale of the investment and hold the net proceeds in trust. Speak with a financial adviser.

19. When does an executor become a trustee?

A personal representative becomes an executor once they complete their duties of collecting all the assets and settling all the estate's debts.

The personal representative then becomes a trustee when they hold the remaining assets until they distribute these in accordance with the will or applicable laws.

Executors also become trustees when they are given temporary ownership of an estate's assets to invest on the behalf of one or more beneficiaries.

20. When does an executor of a will get paid?

An executor is paid at the end of the estate's administration or at the conclusion of the probate when the final accounting is approved and the order is signed by a judge.

However, it is common for friends or family members who are appointed as executors to waive their fees.

21. When should an executor pay beneficiaries?

The executor's first and foremost duty is to settle all debts, liabilities, and taxes of the estate. It is only after all of these liabilities are settled that the residual assets can be distributed with pecuniary legacies (gifts of specific sums of money) taking priority over residuary estate (the remaining money in the estate).

If the will states that a series of payments should be given to a beneficiary, the executor/trustee will make those payments when they fall due.

22. When should an executor notify beneficiaries?

Each province, territory, and state has its own variation of the rules for executors to notify beneficiaries of an estate.

On principle, notification is made once all the assets and liabilities of an estate are established.

However, this may not be all that simple because the executor may need to gather all of this information from banks, land registries, insurance companies, financial investment firms, personal and/or business accountants, lawyers, and financial advisers.

It may take a considerable amount of time to gather all of this information, thereby delaying when the beneficiary notifications can be made.

Additionally, if the will contains a survival clause that has to come into effect, the executor will have to wait for the time specified in the will or by law to elapse before the executor can determine who the valid beneficiaries are who require notification.

23. Who can be an executor of a will?

It is up to the person making the will to decide on an executor or co-executors. It can be a spouse or life partner, sibling, child or children, other family member, corporate executor(s), or a trust company.

While virtually anyone can be chosen as an executor, it is advisable that the executor:

- Lives a reasonably close distance from the person and estate whose will it is.
- Has the presence of mind and patience to deal objectively with relatives, institutions, and beneficiaries.
- Has the time to commit to handling the estate and its affairs.

- Has had prior experience or has the skill set to fill various legal forms.
- Is known to be diligent, honest, have integrity, be fiscally responsible, and have other positive character traits.

24. How much does it cost to remove an executor?

If beneficiaries apply to remove an executor, they may be required to settle from their own finances (rather than the estate) the expenses that the executor incurred while acting in their role.

If the removal requires litigation, there is a chance that a court rules in the executor's favor, in which case the executor's legal fees may have to be paid personally by the challenging beneficiary/beneficiaries, as instructed by the court. Or the fees may be ordered to be paid out of the beneficiary's share of the estate.

It is important to consider the value of the estate before proceeding to attempt to remove an executor through litigation.

If the value of the estate is moderate, it may not be in the beneficiary's interest to pursue a removal by litigation because of the potential loss of time and money that could be incurred.

25. How much is an executor of a will entitled to receive as payment?

A well-drafted will usually specify the method and terms of compensation for the executor's services.

If a will is not available or does not include compensation terms, the courts will rely on the methodology set out by the appropriate regional statutes to determine the amount of compensation.

The principle of most statutes is that an executor's compensation should be fair and reasonable.

To determine fair and reasonable, the courts will look at:

- the value of the estate.

- the complexity of the work in managing and settling the estate.
- the amount of skill required to manage the estate.

The executor may be entitled to additional compensation if the estate's management is significantly complex.

A court may also deduct or cancel the executor's compensation if an executor is deemed to have mismanaged or failed to act promptly in the settling of an estate.

26. How much work is it to be an executor?

The role of an executor comes with a lot of responsibility.

The work involved may be simple and conclude in less than three months if the estate has a sole beneficiary or if the estate's assets will be transferred to a beneficiary without the need for probate, as in the case of jointly owned property.

However, if an estate has disputing beneficiaries, various liabilities, complex assets, and/or requires litigation, the work of an executor may be very difficult and significantly time- and energy-consuming.

If an estate's assets turn out to be too complex for an executor, or seemingly unresolvable disputes erupt among the beneficiaries or with the executor, it is recommended that the executor seek the services of a third-party professional, such as a lawyer, accountant, real estate agent, and/or financial adviser.

27. When do an executor's duties begin?

The executor's duties start before the will is probated.

The executor's duty of preservation of the estate begins immediately after the death of the person whose will it is.

It is not uncommon for an individual who is appointing someone as their executor to inform that person in later life or in the event of serious illness to begin identifying the estate's assets and other required information in anticipation of or preparation for the death of the person whose will it is.

The executor's duties to distribute and settle the estate only take effect after the will's probate in situations where probate is required.

28. When do an executor's duties end?

An executor's duties terminate as soon as they officially remove themselves from the responsibilities or is removed by court order.

Otherwise, an executor's duties end once the final settlement of the estate is filed and the court accepts the account to conclude the order of probate.

In Canada, this occurs when you have the clearance certificate.

In the United States, the probate court will sign off on the final accounting for the estate, after which the executor is officially released from the position.

29. What if I do not want to be the executor of an estate?

Generally, a person named as executor in a will may renounce their appointment as executor.

The renunciation of executorship, unless a court otherwise orders, terminates the executorship of the person renouncing it, and the administration of the estate continues as if the person had never been appointed executor.

Another option may be to forfeit the executorship.

A person appointed as executor may forfeit by not appearing when required to take probate.

This will terminate the executorship and the estate's administration will proceed as if the person had never been appointed.

However, it is important to ensure that you do not interfere with the estate's administration in any material way at any stage if you plan to forfeit the executor's role.

Otherwise, you could be deemed by a court to have indicated your acceptance of the role by your involvement in it.

30. What is the executor process?

Stage 1 – File a petition to begin probate.

Stage 2 – Notify creditors, banks, government, beneficiaries, and heirs.

Stage 3 – Collect all assets, evaluate them, and present a detailed account to the court.

Stage 4 – Settle the estate's liabilities, expenses, and taxes, and obtain a tax clearance certificate from the Canada Revenue Agency. In order to officially close an estate in the United States, you'll need to work with a probate court to finalize the process.

Stage 5 – Distribute residual assets (those remaining after all financial obligations of the estate are paid and acknowledged).

Stage 6 – Close the estate.

31. How do I have to notify the beneficiaries of a will?

The executor of a deceased person may publish a notice in the Newspaper to creditors and other claimants.

32. How does the executor pay each of the beneficiaries of a will?

As noted above, beneficiaries should be paid only after the estate's liabilities and expenses have been settled.

At this stage, a beneficiary may be paid in a variety of ways, depending on terms expressed in the will.

- They may be paid in legacies (financial gifts).
- They may be granted bequests (personal or household belongings as gifts).
- The will may express the wish to establish a trust to pass along the proceeds from the seed assets to specific beneficiaries. In such case, the executor must oversee the establishment of such a trust, and ensure that the appropriate assets are delivered to fund the trust.

- A beneficiary may be left with real estate (such as the principal residence of the deceased).
- The estate's residual assets (those remaining) after all debts, expenses, taxes, bequests, and legacies have been paid, can be distributed by writing to financial institution(s) holding these assets with your request to sell the assets for you to distribute to the beneficiaries or transfer them directly to a sole beneficiary, or to several beneficiaries, as specified in the will.

Regardless of how beneficiaries are paid or how the estate is distributed, make sure that all the beneficiaries provide you with a written acknowledgment that they have received their disbursements from the estate. This could be in the form of a signed hand-delivered note, mailed letter, or email.

33. Under what circumstances might a beneficiary challenge the executor of a will?

A beneficiary might challenge an executor if the beneficiary considers or knows an executor to be:

- incapable of managing their own affairs, let alone the estate.
- has been convicted of an offense involving dishonesty.
- is an undischarged bankrupt (legally bankrupt but still having to pay back certain debts and unable to borrow money from a bank without disclosing the bankruptcy).
- not responsive to communications by letter, email, or phone.
- otherwise unwilling or unable to carry out the duties of a personal representative to an extent that the conduct of the personal representative hampers the efficient administration of the estate.
- unreasonably refuses to carry out the duties of a personal representative.

Beneficiaries who are disappointed with their designated share of an estate may challenge the validity of the will or bring forth a claim for greater provision.

34. What do I do if a beneficiary challenges my role as the executor?

As executor, you should adopt a neutral stance even if challenged. If you are also a beneficiary, can you defend your entitlement?

If you are one of several co-executors, not all of whom are beneficiaries, it is sometimes better for you to be represented by your own lawyer. Solicitors cannot act on behalf of all the beneficiaries if there is a deemed or potential conflict of interest.

Occasionally, if involved parties are at an impasse, it can become inappropriate or too risky to continue as an executor.

In such circumstances, it might be wise to have a neutral candidate be appointed in your place as executor as agreed upon by all of the beneficiaries and/or decided by a court.

As family members are not always ideally suited or deemed to be neutral, it is often best for this replacement as executor to be a solicitor.

This has its advantages, but it will likely be costly, and whether this is the best solution depends very much on the estate's value. You don't want an estate's modest funds to all go toward paying a lawyer or other appointed professional.

35. What do you do if a beneficiary of a will is deceased?

In general, when a designated beneficiary dies before the person who left them a benefit in a will passes away, that gift fails. The former beneficiary's estate does not receive anything from the other estate.

However, if beneficiaries survive a will's deceased but then die before receiving their inheritance, usually this inheritance will form part of their estate to be passed on to their beneficiaries according to their will or the rules of intestacy (the rules that apply when a person dies without having a valid will in force).

36. What information is the beneficiary of a will entitled to obtain?

A beneficiary should promptly be informed of their entitlement under a will.

If there is no will, the beneficiaries should be informed of their entitlement according to the deceased's intestacy (the rules governing the distribution of an estate in the absence of a will).

When beneficiaries are not informed of their entitlement within a reasonable time, the law provides all beneficiaries with certain rights to access information relating to their entitlement. Those rights include a right to receive a copy of the will.

For a beneficiary to effectively monitor the administration of estate property, the beneficiary needs information regarding the performance of the executor's duties and powers.

To this end, the law has imposed on executors and trustees a duty to account for the estate's processing to beneficiaries.

However, the nature of the beneficiary's interest can dictate the extent of information to which a beneficiary is entitled.

A beneficiary who holds an interest in a specific asset (such as a boat or a bank account) has a right to access information in relation to that specific asset, but generally nothing more.

The right to be informed of the expected date of distribution and any delay that may be occasioned must also be conveyed to all beneficiaries.

Beneficiaries must also be advised of any litigation against the estate that may affect their entitlement under the will or intestacy.

37. When should a beneficiary get a copy of the will?

Before probate of a will is granted, only the executor or co-executors of the will are entitled to read it. It will be at the discretion of the executor or co-executors whether to share it with the beneficiary as a matter of courtesy.

Sometimes the non-probated will is kept from the beneficiaries in case it is superseded by another more recent will, or put in dispute by another document prepared by the deceased or presented by an interested party.

Once probate is granted and the executor or co-executors have undertaken the process of distributing the estate, a copy of the will should be given to any beneficiary who has requested it.

A will becomes public information after probate. At that point, a beneficiary can simply request a copy of the will from the Probate Registry.

38. Who cannot be a beneficiary of a will?

A person who is not named in a will to receive all or part of an estate cannot be a beneficiary of that will.

If there is no will, only a spouse and/or a spouse and the descendants of the deceased can be the beneficiaries of an estate.

If the person who made the will has no surviving spouse or surviving descendants upon death, some courts may rule that the estate is to be divided among the intestate's surviving parents, descendants of the parents, or grandparents or great-grandparents.

If the person who made the will has no living relatives, then the estate may be given to the government.

It is important to note that former spouses may not be the beneficiaries of an estate unless they are specifically mentioned as beneficiaries in their current unmarried state.

Beneficiaries who predecease the person who made the will may not be beneficiaries of the estate.

Any individual found to be criminally responsible for the death of the person who made the will may not be a beneficiary of the estate.

Witnesses to the will's signing cannot be a beneficiary.

It is important to note that pets cannot be beneficiaries.

39. What are the rights of a beneficiary?

A beneficiary is entitled to:

- be notified by an executor of their entitlement to gifts from a will.
- obtain a copy of a will once it is probated.
- request/apply to remove an executor.
- challenge the validity of a will.
- ask for accountability regarding an executor's management of an estate.

40. What are the questions that executors should ask when they find out that they've been named as an executor or co-executor?

The questions will vary because every single estate is unique. The regulations that govern them also differ regionally throughout Canada. However, some basic questions are:

- Where is the will kept?
- Does the will require probate?
- Where are the documents to the estate's assets kept?
- What is the value of the estate?
- What is the value of the individual assets?
- Does the newly deceased have regular expenses that need to be stopped (such as a gym or yacht club membership, utilities, cable, and other subscription services)?
- Does the newly deceased have credit cards with amounts owing?
- Where are the beneficiaries? Is their contact information available (addresses, phone numbers, email addresses)?
- Do I need professional assistance to help with the estate's settlement?
- Do I have the time to be an executor?

41. What are the executor's responsibilities?

The executor is responsible for:

- initiating or defending actions as the person whose will it is would have done, if still living, according to the laws of where they lived.
- actions for wrongs done to or by the deceased person whose will it is.
- handling any actions in which the deceased person whose will it is was named as a defendant.
- remedying unpaid rentals to the property owners.
- initiating and maintaining actions to recover damages and costs for a trespass done to the estate, goods, credits or effects of the person whose will it is during his or her lifetime, in the same manner that the deceased, if living, would have initiated or maintained.
- debts relating to the estate.
- raising money when the will had no expressed provision for settling debts.

42. What are the responsibilities of the executor of a trust?

The role of the executor of a trust can be expensive and time-consuming.

An executor is responsible for the administration and protection of the trustee's estate.

The role will require the collection of assets, tax compliance responsibilities, and the collection of proceeds from the assets held in the estate.

The executor is also responsible for executing certain tasks on behalf of a trustee, such as managing education costs, living expenses, legal issues, or ensuring that an estate that holds interests in businesses is run prudently and efficiently.

Being the executor of a trust requires making sound and accountable financial judgments.

43. How do I prove that am the executor of an estate?

A well-drafted will clearly states the name of the appointed executor (or co-executors). Besides the will, an executor will normally be given written authority to act on behalf of the estate by a lawyer.

44. Who appoints the executor of an estate?

The person whose will it is appoints the executor in his or her will?

In the event that there is no will or if the named executor for whatever reason either refuses or is removed from that role, the court may appoint an executor to act on behalf of the estate and/or a trust from the estate.

45. How do I report executor fees in my tax filing?

Executor fees are considered to be income from an office or employment. Accordingly, they must be reported on a T4 slip in Canada. The IRS in the United States says these fees are to be reported as gross income.

46. What can an executor claim for expenses?

Executors can claim expense fees for costs that are warranted or substantiated.

For a court to award an executor compensation beyond core compensation, the executor must demonstrate the exertion of effort beyond that already accounted for by core compensation.

If provided examples of additional effort—such as complexities in the administration of the estate or a trust arising from the nature of the assets, taxation problems, numerous categories of beneficiaries, or litigation by or against the estate—additional compensation may be granted.

A court will not award compensation for activities that an executor claims require additional compensation if these have already been taken into account by the award for core compensation.

Executors can claim expense fees for costs that are warranted or substantiated.

47. How do I handle bank account(s)?

When you have informed the financial institutions you are the executor, the accounts will be frozen and most transactions may only be processed with your approval.

Financial institutions will allow certain payments, such as funeral expenses, payments necessary for maintaining certain assets, and expenses related to the administration of the estate.

The allowance of other payments will depend on the financial institution.

You should also ask the financial institutions for lists of past transactions in the bank accounts and credit card accounts. This will assist in identifying the various accounts.

48. What is an estate bank account?

This is a bank account you must open in the name of the estate. You must also close the decedent's bank account. You should never co-mingle your own money with the money of the estate.

49. How do banks discover someone died?

Banks can discover the death of an account holder in a few ways. Funeral directors will take on the task of informing Social Security of a person's death on behalf of the family. In Canada, you provide documents that prove you are executor.

50. What happens to joint accounts when someone dies?

Most joint bank accounts include automatic rights of survivorship.

This means if one of the signers on the account passes away, the remaining signer (or signers) on the account retain ownership of the money in the account.

That means that the surviving account owner can continue using the account, and the money in it, without any interruptions.

Resources Page

I have a great list of resources that will help you learn more on a variety of topics covered in this book. I've even included a few sources of consultants and suppliers that may be of help to you.

However, because I am constantly finding new material and people, it makes sense to move this list online.

I update it regularly visit it anytime.

www.davidedey.com/resources

There is no registration or password needed.

I think you will be impressed. Other readers stop by often and have frequently made excellent suggestions for me to check out and potentially add.

Thanks for your interest and for taking the time to read *Executor Help* I really appreciate it

Wouldn't someone or a group you know benefit from reading Executor Help?

It makes a great gift, one that you'll be thanked for because you are keeping families together.

You know the book is understandable, fun to read and most of all practical. If you would like to do a bulk order, go to: www.davidedey.com

If you have any questions, please feel free to reach out or if you would like me to speak to your group or association let me know. Contact me at: david@davidedey.com

CPSIA information can be obtained
at www.ICGtesting.com
Printed in the USA
LVHW101921111121
703086LV00007B/8/J